52BIBLE
CHARACTERS
Dramatized

Books by Kenneth W. Osbeck

25 Most Treasured Gospel Hymn Stories
52 Bible Characters Dramatized
52 Hymn Stories Dramatized
101 Hymn Stories
101 More Hymn Stories
Amazing Grace: 366 Hymn Stories for Personal Devotions
Beyond the Sunset
Devotional Warm-Ups for the Church Choir
Hallelujah, What a Savior
Joy to the World
The Ministry of Music
Pocket Guide for the Church Choir Member
A Song for All Seasons

52 BIBLE CHARACTERS
Dramatized

**Easy-to-Use Monologues
for All Occasions**

Kenneth W. Osbeck

kregel
PUBLICATIONS

Grand Rapids, MI 49501

52 Bible Characters Dramatized

© 1996 by Kenneth W. Osbeck

Published by Kregel Publications, a division of Kregel, Inc., P.O. Box 2607, Grand Rapids, MI 49501. Kregel Publications provides trusted, biblical publications for Christian growth and service. Your comments and suggestions are valued.

Cover photo: Copyright © 1996 Kregel, Inc.
Cover and book design: Alan G. Hartman

Library of Congress Cataloging-in-Publication Data
Osbeck, Kenneth W.
   52 Bible characters dramatized / by Kenneth W. Osbeck.
     p.   cm.
   1. Bible—Biography. 2. Christian drama, American.
3. Bible plays. 4. Monologues I. Title.
BS571.077   1996   220.9'.2—dc20   95-33432
                                            CIP

ISBN 0-8254-3429-7

3 4 5 6 / 04

Printed in the United States of America

Contents

OLD TESTAMENT

NEW TESTAMENT

WOMEN OF THE BIBLE

MEN OF THE BIBLE

Preface

Much of the Bible pertains to people and their relationships. More than three thousand specific names of individuals are recorded throughout Scripture. Relating the past experiences of others to our own lives enables us to have the foresight to trust God more explicitly and thereby know the meaning of "abundant living" and the promise of eternal life. These biblical people also teach us important insights about God—His character, attributes, and the way He moves in the lives of people and nations. The Bible states that these examples of the past have been written for our benefit "so that through endurance and the encouragement of the Scriptures we might have hope" (Rom. 15:4; 1 Cor. 10:6, 11).

We must never lose an appreciation of our heritage and the blessings of the past. Our faith is built on historical facts, and we are surrounded by a "great cloud of witnesses" (Heb. 12:1). During the sixteenth century Protestant Reformation Movement, the Bible was established as the supreme authority, and congregational singing was restored to the people. Since then evangelical congregations have rightly been labeled as "people of two books"—the infallible Scriptures, through which God has communicated His eternal truths, and the hymnal, with which believers have responded with worthy expressions of "psalms, hymns and spiritual songs."

The purpose of *52 Hymn Stories Dramatized* and *52 Bible Characters Dramatized* is to encourage congregations to return to the basics—a renewed awareness of the Bible and the church hymnal's importance in their worship services. Group singing can be greatly enhanced by having several people use *52 Hymn Stories Dramatized* to introduce brief but informative background sketches of favorite hymns. These fifty-two Bible monologues have various possible uses.

1. As devotional reading—they can be especially useful to believers as an enlightening overview of the Bible by introducing a number of its important characters.
2. As a regular special feature in a worship service in the same way a musical selection is used.
3. As an integral part of the sermon or lesson.
4. As a creative basis for an entire program—in Sunday school sessions or in meetings for men, women, seniors, and youth—with the use of other related activities such as music and discussions.

With either of these publications, the performance can be given as simply or elaborately as desired. The script may be read or can be given from memory with appropriate costumes and props. Since young people today generally enjoy dramatic activities, these monologues provide excellent opportunities for their involvement in a public service. Christian schools will find these materials useful for classes in expression and communication.

It would also be helpful to include in the church bulletin the Scripture reference and a brief spiritual reflection or application for each monologue. A short summary of a related hymn's background might be of interest as well. Information about most of these suggested hymns can be found in *101 Hymn Stories* and *101 More Hymn Stories*.

The more we understand God's grace, the more we desire to respond to Him in worship and praise. Learning to worship in "spirit and truth" should be a believer's lifetime pursuit. May we continue this important quest by making an even greater use of the companion books essential for our spiritual maturity—the inspired Holy Bible and the church hymnal.

—Kenneth W. Osbeck

About the Osbecks

Since their retirement from teaching, Ken and Betty Osbeck have shared their dramatized hymn story and Bible character programs with more than five-hundred church groups throughout the Midwest. God has greatly blessed this ministry and has made it a spiritually enriching time in their own lives. The Osbecks were formerly teachers in the Grand Rapids area, at the Grand Rapids School of the Bible and Music and the Grand Rapids Baptist College and Seminary (now merged as Cornerstone College and Baptist Seminary)—Ken in church music and the fine arts and Betty in speech and drama. They both hold graduate degrees from the University of Michigan. Ken has also served as music director in seven area churches and for the Radio Bible Class, Children's Bible Hour, and Youth for Christ. He is the author of a number of books for the church music ministry, all published by Kregel Publications. The Osbecks are members of Calvary Church and have four grown children and two granddaughters.

OLD TESTAMENT

Drama 1

Eve

Walk in all the ways I command you that it may go well with you (Jeremiah 7:23).

The Garden of Eden was truly a perfect paradise. It was filled with everything one could possibly desire—flowing rivers, abundant fruits and vegetables, beautiful trees and flowers. When God created my husband Adam and me and placed us in that delightful place, we lived in happy innocence. Often in the cool of the day, God Himself would come and visit with us. All that He asked was that we maintain the beauty of His creation.

In the center of the garden was a special tree called the *Tree of Life*. There was also a second tree called the *Tree of Knowledge of Good and Evil*. I was especially intrigued by this one. But my husband had often instructed me that God told him we could eat freely from every tree in the garden except the *Tree of Knowledge of Good and Evil*. If we disobeyed we would in that day surely die!

One day a serpent, the craftiest of all the animals in the garden, approached me as I was peacefully resting in view of this forbidden tree. It tempted me to merely taste the tree's unusual fruit. I was fearful and told the serpent that Jehovah Himself had forbidden it, and if we disobeyed we would surely die!

"You shall not surely die!" said the cunning serpent boldly. "God knows that when you eat of this fruit, your eyes will be opened, and you will be like God Himself, knowing both good and evil."

I looked longingly at the appealing fruit. I could see that it was pleasant to the eye and certainly would taste good. I believed that if I took some and ate, I truly would become wiser. There did not seem to be any harm in at least trying it. My desire grew stronger as I pondered this . . . and finally,

12

I decided to take one small bite. After I had done so, I offered a taste to Adam and he ate of it also. Immediately everything about us seemed different! Since for some reason we began to feel embarrassed with each other, we quickly sewed fig leaves together to cover our bodies. Soon evening came with its cool refreshing breezes, but for the first time we were stricken with fear as we heard God's footsteps approaching.

"Adam, where are you?" We tried hiding among the trees when we heard God's voice. "Have you eaten of the tree from which I commanded you not to eat?" My husband responded meekly that I had given him the fruit. Timidly I explained to God that I was deceived by the serpent.

"Because you have done this," God told the serpent, "cursed are you above all the livestock and all the wild animals! I will put enmity between you and the woman, and between your offspring and hers; he will crush your head, and you will strike his heel."

Then the Lord God turned to me. "I will greatly increase your pains in childbearing; with pain you will give birth to children. And Adam, because you listened to your wife and ate from the tree about which I commanded you, cursed is the ground because of you. . . . By the sweat of your brow you will eat your food until you return to the ground, since from it you were taken. Dust you are and to dust you will return."

Before we were banished from the garden, God once more showed His loving kindness by clothing us with special garments made of skins. He warned, however, that we could never again return to Eden nor enjoy the Tree of Life with its promise of immortality. Our hearts were heavy that day as we left the beautiful home we had lost because of disobedience. When we turned for one last look, we saw an angel with a flaming sword guarding the Tree of Life.

Soon I gave birth to our first son, whom we named Cain. How joyful we were to be able with the Lord's help to bring forth another person like ourselves. God kept blessing our family with many more sons and daughters. The anguish and pain of childbearing were soon forgotten with the thrill of each new life.

My years have been filled with remorse for my early

disobedience to God, and my heart has often been heavy with the grief He has allowed me to endure. Still I find much comfort in the many children I have been privileged to bear and in the promise that I will be known to future generations as the "mother of all the living." Blessed be our Jehovah God!

****

Scripture References:
> Genesis 2:8–25; 3

Spiritual Reflections:
> Truths to Ponder:
> - The significance of the two trees
> - The character of God
> - The garments of skin
> - The appeal of the temptation:
>   - Sensual—the forbidden fruit was pleasant to the eye.
>   - Physical—it appeared tasteful.
>   - Intellectual—they would become wiser.
>   (See 2 Cor. 11:3; James 1: 12–15)

Suggested Hymns:
> - "How Great Thou Art"
> - "This Is My Father's World"

Noah

> By faith Noah . . . condemned the world and became
> heir of the righteousness that comes by faith (Hebrews
> 11:7).

The world had become such a miserable place! I grew deeply
discouraged. For many years I had been much disturbed by
the shameful wickedness of the people all around me. The
thoughts and imaginations of every individual were
continually evil and violent. Year after year I told them to
repent of their sinful ways and follow after Jehovah and His
paths of righteousness. But my words were scoffed at and
ignored. In fact, there were many times when I thought the
people might even kill me because of their resentment to my
preaching.

Then one day, while communing with God, I was
astounded to hear Him declare: "I am going to put an end
to all people, for the earth is filled with violence because of
them. I am surely going to destroy both them and the earth."

The Lord revealed that I was to build an ark as a place of
refuge for my wife and me, as well as our three sons and
their wives. I was to continue to preach, but unless others
repented, from the entire earth only we eight people would
be saved. God gave me very specific instructions for the
building of this ark. It was to be made of cypress wood,
covered inside and out with pitch, and divided into a number
of small compartments. It was to be 450 feet long, 75 feet
wide, and 45 feet high, with three tiers that reached within
18 inches of the top. A door was to be made on the side with
provisions for letting in light. The Lord also instructed that
in addition to my immediate family, I was to take two of all
living creatures, male and female. To keep them alive I was
to store food for everyone.

For more than 100 years I worked diligently on this ark,

always mindful of the exact instructions God had given. How the people laughed and jeered as I labored on with never a sight of rain. The work was detailed and difficult, but at last the task was finished! My wife and I, our three sons—Shem, Ham and Japheth (JA-feth)—and their wives entered the ark with all the living creatures. And then God shut the door! Nothing happened for seven long days. But suddenly rain began to fall and it seemed as if the very windows of heaven had opened. For forty days the downpour continued. The rising flood waters lifted the ark high above the mountains, and for 150 days the mighty waters covered the earth.

At last God sent over the earth a great wind which caused the waters to steadily recede. Then we felt the ark settle on the top of a mountain range, and from there I could see the other large mountains around us gradually become visible. After another 40 days, I opened a window and sent out a raven to test for dry ground. The bird never returned. Later I sent out a dove, but the bird soon flew back to me since it could find no dry place on which to land. After seven more days, when I released the dove, it returned with a freshly plucked olive leaf in its beak. Then I knew that the water had begun to dry up. When I sent the dove out once more and it didn't return, I felt certain that now the earth was able to provide the nourishment these creatures needed for survival.

At God's command, I came out with my family and all of the living creatures. What a joyous celebration that was! As quickly as possible I built an altar to the Lord for all His goodness to us. Taking several of our finest creatures, I sacrificed a burnt offering on the altar. Later God revealed to me that He was pleased with our sacrifice of worship. He said that He would never again curse the earth because of man, even though man's inclinations are evil from childhood. "As long as the earth endures," He promised, "seedtime and harvest, cold and heat, summer and winter, day and night will never cease."

God blessed our family and told us to be fruitful and replenish the earth. Much as He had done for Adam and Eve, our first parents, God gave us dominion over all the earth, its creatures, and the fish of the sea. As a continual reminder of His promise that He would never again destroy the earth with a flood, God declared, "I have set my rainbow in the clouds. . . . This is the sign of the covenant I have established between Me and all life on the earth."

Through the many years since the flood, God has blessed me with an abundant life. I have walked in daily fellowship with Him in all of life's experiences. Now I am anticipating spending a glorious eternity in His righteous presence. Blessed be our covenant keeping God!

* * * *

Scripture References:
   Genesis 6:3–22; 7:1–8; 9:10; 2 Peter 2:5

Spiritual Reflections:
   Noah is a vivid example of living a righteous life in a corrupt environment— "a righteous man, blameless in his generation" (Gen. 6:9).

   "As it was in the days of Noah, so it will be at the coming of the Son of man" (Matt. 24:37–38).

Suggested Hymns:
   • "O for a Closer Walk with God"
   • "May the Mind of Christ, My Savior"

Drama 3

Abraham

Abraham believed God, and it was credited to him as righteousness, and he was called God's friend (James 2:23).

In the mighty Babylonian Empire, the famous city of Ur lies along the Euphrates (u-FRA-tez) River, not far from the Persian Gulf. It was here that I grew up. My father, Terah (TE-rah), was a wealthy and influential leader in the city. In this pagan country the sun and moon are the principal objects of worship; yet my family, as direct descendants of Noah's son Shem, had been taught that the God of our ancestors— Jehovah—was the One true God. We believed that He alone was worthy of our worship.

After my marriage to beautiful Sarah, my father felt that because our city was threatened with an invasion, it was wise for our entire family to leave. He chose a place called Haran (Ha-ran), an important commercial region that lay between Egypt and Damascus. We set out with all of our flocks and possessions and settled happily in our new land. There I lived until my father's death. It was here that we buried him with great honor.

Shortly after this, I was startled when God spoke to me personally. "Leave your country, your people and your father's household, Abraham, and go to the land I will show you. I will make you into a great nation and I will bless you; I will make your name great, and you will be a blessing. I will bless those who bless you, and whoever curses you I will curse. All the people on earth will be blessed through you."

I was astonished, but with God's promises ringing in my mind, I made preparations immediately to move, even though I did not know with certainty where I was to go. I only knew that God had spoken, and I desired to obey His

18

voice. With my faithful wife Sarah at my side, I also took my brother's son Lot and his family as traveling companions. All went well for a time as we traveled southward. Soon, however, quarreling began between my herdsmen and those of my nephew over the best grazing lands for our individual flocks. I tried to keep peace by telling Lot that as kinsmen we should not be quarreling like that. Finally, it seemed best that we part company. I told my nephew to look out over all the lands before us and make his choice. If he wanted to go to the right or left, I would go the opposite way. As we stood on the hills of Bethel (BETH-el), my nephew could see among many fertile valleys the city of Sodom, known for its widespread wickedness. Lot made his choice. He took his flocks, his wife, and his young daughters and set out for their new life in the sinful city.

Soon I heard the voice of God once again: "Lift up your eyes from where you are, Abraham, and look north and south, east and west. All the land that you see I will give to you and your offspring forever. I will make your heirs like the dust of the earth, so that if anyone could count the dust, then your offspring could be counted. So walk through the length and breadth of the land, for I am giving it to you."

Though I knew that God had promised this, in my heart I questioned how this could ever be since Sarah and I had no sons, and we were both beyond the childbearing years. But then God reassured me, "I will bless Sarah and will surely give you a son by her. You will call his name Isaac. I will establish with him an everlasting covenant for his descendants."

How thrilled Sarah and I were when God gave us our son. When the time came for him to be weaned, I had a festive feast prepared in his honor. Isaac continued to delight us through the years, and we never ceased giving thanks to God for His faithfulness in blessing us with this special son.

But one day I was shaken by God's command: "Take your son, your only son Isaac, whom you love, and go to the region of Moriah (mo-RI-ah). Sacrifice him there as a burnt offering on one of the mountains I will tell you about." But how could this be? Surely it must be a mistake! I knew that among our pagan neighbors it was a common practice for a family to offer their oldest son to a particular deity even if it meant a human sacrifice. But why would Jehovah God ask this of us after giving His promise that our descendants would one day become a great nation?

Even though I felt greatly confused, I realized that I must obey the voice of the Lord. In spite of this disturbing command, I knew that I must have faith that God would remain true to His eternal promise. Early the next morning, without saying a word to anyone, I rose and saddled my donkey, awakened Isaac, and took two young men along as helpers. We carried a supply of wood for the sacrifice and set forth for Mount Moriah. On the third day we arrived at the mountain. I told my servants, "Stay here with the donkey while the boy and I go over there. We will worship and then we will come back to you."

As Isaac and I walked along, he carried the wood and I the fire and knife. I was deeply anguished when he asked, "Father, behold the fire and the wood, but where is the lamb for a burnt offering?" With tears clouding my eyes, I replied, "God Himself will provide the lamb, my son." We continued our walk quietly together. When we reached the spot that God had told me about, I built an altar and arranged the wood on it. With a heavy heart, I bound Isaac, my only son, and laid him on the wood. As I stretched out my hand with the knife to slay him, a voice from heaven shouted, "Abraham! Abraham! Do not lay a hand on the boy. Do not do anything to him. Now I know that you fear God, because you have not withheld from Me your son, your only son."

I dropped the knife, unbound my son and embraced him dearly! Looking up I saw a ram caught in the thicket of a nearby bush. With gratitude I sacrificed it as a burnt offering instead of my son. I called the spot Jehovah-Jireh (JI-reh)—"A Place Where the Lord Will Provide."

God's voice came a second time: "Because you have done this, Abraham, and have not withheld your only son, I will surely bless you and make your descendants as numerous as the stars in the sky and as the sand on the seashore. Your descendants will take possession of the cities of their enemies. Through your offspring all nations on earth will be blessed because you have obeyed Me."

Isaac and I returned to our two young servants. Together we journeyed to our home in Beersheba (beer-SHE-bah), greatly rejoicing in the goodness of our Jehovah God and His faithfulness to those who truly obey His commands.

∗ ∗ ∗ ∗

Scripture References:
   Genesis 12–25; Galatians 3:7–9, 16; Hebrews 11:8–19

Spiritual Reflections:
   Abraham is called the "father of a multitude of nations" (Gen. 17:4). With the exception of Moses, Abraham is mentioned more times in the New Testament than any other Old Testament figure. Read Romans 4 for a New Testament interpretation of Abraham's faith. Note the apostle Paul's argument that faith as it was demonstrated by Abraham has always been more important to salvation than keeping the Mosaic Law.

> The highest joy that can be known
>   by those who heav'nward wend
> Is the Word of Life to own,
>   and God to have as friend.
>   —Nils Frykman

Suggested Hymns:
   • "The God of Abraham Praise"
   • "My Faith Looks Up to Thee"

Drama 4

Rebekah

Houses and wealth are inherited from parents, but a
prudent wife is from the Lord (Proverbs 19:14).

It was late afternoon as I made my way to the well outside
our city of Haran (HA-ran) in the land of Syria. Here each
day the women and girls of the town gathered to obtain
water for their families' evening use. As I approached the
well, I was surprised to see an impressive looking stranger
resting there with his flock of camels and helpers. Since he
looked so weary, I offered him a cool drink as well as water
for his animals and attendants. Politely he asked my name.
"Rebekah," I answered timidly, "the daughter of Bethuel
(be-THU-el), who is a nephew of Father Abraham."

The stranger seemed especially pleased at our meeting.
He introduced himself as Eliezer (el-i-E zer) and said that he
was Father Abraham's trusted servant. After bowing his head
in prayer, he proceeded to present me with several costly
gifts. I was overwhelmed. Later he asked if there was a
possibility that he and his group might have a night's lodging
at our home. I assured him that we had plenty of food and
supplies for everyone. As quickly as I could, I ran home to
tell my family about this unusual man who had traveled a
long distance from our esteemed Great Uncle Abraham's
home.

My brother Laban (LA-ban), hearing my account, returned
hurriedly to the well and led Eliezer and his helpers to our
home, where we made them all welcome. Before eating the
evening meal, however, Eliezer insisted that he must first
tell us the purpose of his visit. We listened with rapt attention
as he told about Abraham and Sarah and how God had
blessed them with great prosperity. In their old age Jehovah
had miraculously given them a son named Isaac . . . and
now that their son was grown, the time had come for him to

take a wife. Eliezer had been sent on this long journey to seek a wife for Isaac among Abraham's family. While resting and praying about this matter at our well, Eliezer had it revealed to him that I was the young maiden God had chosen.

My family responded thoughtfully, "This is from the Lord. We can say nothing to you one way or the other. Here is Rebekah . . . take her and go, and let her become the wife of your master's son, as the Lord has directed."

Father Abraham was a name much revered by our God-fearing family. We had been taught that Jehovah had promised to develop a great nation from Abraham's seed, and that one day all the earth would be blessed through his heirs. Though it saddened me to leave my dear family, I answered, "I am willing to leave with Eliezer on the long journey south to become Isaac's wife."

Soon after our joyous marriage, Isaac and I began praying for a family, a heritage of the Lord. After twenty years of patient waiting, we had our faith in Jehovah's covenant with Father Abraham rewarded. The Lord God spoke to me, confirming His promise, "Two nations are in your womb, and two peoples from within you will be separated; one people will be stronger than the other, and the older will serve the younger."

In time I gave birth to twin boys, Esau, the first born . . . then Jacob. We loved our two sons dearly. As they grew older, however, it became apparent that they were complete opposites of each other. Esau, who was rough and robust, loved the outdoors and became a skillful hunter. Jacob was quiet, thoughtful and very clever, usually enjoying life at home. As time went on, my husband became more attached to Esau while my affections were drawn to Jacob. Somehow I sensed that he had the qualities necessary for continuing the eternal promise given to Father Abraham.

Coldness and distance developed between our two sons. Their animosity toward each other as well as our personal favoritisms led to a growing separation between Isaac and me as well. One day when Esau returned home, completely famished from an extended hunting trip, Jacob gave him food in exchange for his birthright, which had never really been appreciated by Esau. Then on another occasion, I happened to overhear his father tell Esau to hunt for some special game that my husband particularly relished and by doing so receive Isaac's eternal blessing. I was determined that since Jacob was more worthy than Esau, he should receive this blessing. Knowing that Isaac's eyes had become dim with age, I devised a plan to deceive my husband.

But Jacob was fearful when I told him to dress in Esau's clothing and pretend that he was his brother when appearing before his father. I assured my son that I would take full responsibility for this scheme. I dressed Jacob in furs so that he looked and felt like Esau. My husband proceeded to give Jacob this blessing: "May God give you of heaven's dew and earth's richness—an abundance of grain and new wine. May nations serve you and peoples bow down to you. . . . May those who curse you be cursed and those who bless you be blessed."

No sooner had Jacob left than Esau appeared from his hunting trip. After preparing the tasty food for his father, he requested the promised blessing. Esau was furious when he realized that he had been outwitted once again by Jacob. "He has deceived me these two times," he shouted. "He took my birthright and now he's taken my blessing."

Esau angrily vowed that as soon as his father was dead, he would surely kill his brother. When I heard this threat, I urged Jacob to flee from our home immediately and take refuge in my homeland with my brother Laban. Before Jacob left, my husband once again reaffirmed his blessing. He also advised our son that he should choose a wife from his mother's family when he arrived in Haran.

With great sorrow and secrecy, we sent Jacob on his way to Haran. I thought he would be gone for just a brief time until Esau's anger had subsided . . . but now many years have passed and I have never seen my beloved son. Though my heart is often heavy because of this, I rest in the eternal promise. It gives me the assurance that Jacob will have an important place in Jehovah's plan of blessing given to Father Abraham and my husband Isaac. For this I will always be grateful to God.

* * * *

Scripture References:

Genesis 22:20–24; 24; 25:19–34; 27; 28:1–5; 29:12; 32; Romans 9:10–13; Hebrews 11:20

Spiritual Reflections:

What causes a parent to sometimes favor one child over another? Can Rebekah's deceitful actions be justified by her noble intentions?

Suggested Hymns:

- "Dear Lord and Father of Mankind"
- "Children of the Heavenly Father"

Drama 5

Jacob

The Lord . . . will send His angel with you and make
your journey a success (Genesis 24:40).

We were twins, Esau and I . . . but how strange that we
should be so different in many ways. Esau was an
outdoorsman, very fond of hunting and adventure. I
preferred quieter activities and sociability with my family
and friends. Although my brother was skilled in physical
pursuits, I was considered to be more creative and clever.
Perhaps that was why I succeeded in outwitting Esau at
times. Since he was born shortly before me, he possessed
the special privileges of a first-born. With careful scheming,
however, I was able to change this so that his rightful
birthright belonged to me. When our father Isaac became
nearly blind, I was disguised as Esau and thereby also gained
the parental blessing intended for him.

Because of these special favors that I stole from him, Esau
vowed to kill me! It was necessary for me to make sudden
plans to escape from our home in Beersheba (beer-SHE-bah).
My parents urged me to make my way immediately to the
land of Syria, to the village of Haran (HA-ran), where my
mother's brother Laban (LA-ban) and his household lived.

I knew it would be a very long trip, so on that first day I
went as far as I could before collapsing from exhaustion. I took
a stone and used it for a pillow. But I had the most unusual
dream! I saw a ladder stretching from earth to heaven with
God's angels ascending and descending on it. At the top of the
ladder stood the Lord Himself saying to me, "I am the Lord,
the God of Abraham and your father Isaac." To my amazement,
Jehovah made the same promise to me that He had previously
made to my father and grandfather: that our descendants would
be blessed and in turn would be a blessing to all the families
of the earth. Then the Almighty made this vow: "I am with

you, Jacob, and will watch over you wherever you go . . . I will not leave you until I have done what I have promised you."

When I awoke from my sleep, I felt shaken! "This is none other than the house of God," I exclaimed. I took the stone that I had placed under my head and set it up as a pillar, poured oil on it, and began worshiping and renewing my vows to the Lord. I called the place Bethel (BETH-el)—"the house of God." From that time on I had the assurance that I was destined to fulfill God's eternal promise.

For many days I traveled northward to Haran. When I finally approached the village, in a nearby field I saw a well with several flocks of sheep waiting for their watering time. I asked the attending shepherds if they knew my Uncle Laban. While we were talking, his young daughter Rachel arrived with her sheep. I introduced myself to her and proceeded to help her with the watering chores. I was so overcome by the gracious beauty of this young relative that I kissed her and began to weep with joy. She ran home immediately and told her father about my arrival. As soon as Laban heard this news, he warmly welcomed me to his household, explaining that I was one of his own flesh and blood.

For the next month I was treated as a guest in my uncle's home. I always tried, however, to make myself useful to him by working with his flocks and herds. At the end of this time, my uncle was so pleased with my work that he insisted I stay on. He asked what wages I would like for continuing my services with him. I had already made up my mind that when Rachel was old enough, I wanted her as my bride. I knew that it was customary to give the bride's parents a handsome dowry when asking for their daughter in marriage. Since I had nothing to offer, I proposed that I would continue working without wages for the next seven years in order to win the younger daughter as my wife. Uncle Laban readily agreed to this bargain. For the next seven years I worked faithfully in my uncle's service; yet because of my tender love for Rachel, the time seemed like only a few days.

At last the wedding day arrived. A great feast was prepared for this festive occasion and I was full of joy. But the next morning my joy was turned to anger when I discovered that my uncle had deceived me. He had disguised his oldest daughter Leah (LE-ah) to appear as Rachel. I had married the wrong daughter, and she was as unpleasant to the eye as Rachel was lovely.

"What is this you have done to me?" I shouted to my uncle. "I served you for Rachel, didn't I? Why have you deceived me?"

My uncle explained that it was always the custom to have the oldest daughter married before the younger one. He bargained, "Finish Leah's bridal week . . . then we will give you the younger one also in return for another seven years of work." Presently I had two wives, though Rachel was always my first love. As I continued working for my uncle another seven years, the Lord did not see fit to bless Rachel with any children while Leah bore me six sons and one daughter. Finally, however, God heard Rachel's fervent prayer, and she gave birth to a handsome son, whom we named Joseph. I loved this boy dearly.

After Joseph's birth, I asked my uncle to send me on my way so that I could return to my homeland. Laban pleaded with me not to leave, offering any wages I desired. We finally agreed that I would stay on in exchange for a portion of the weaker animals from his flock.

During the next six years, as my smaller flock prospered, Laban and his sons grew increasingly envious. Then the Lord told me that this was the time for me to return to the land of my father Isaac, whom I had learned was still alive. The next day, while Laban was away shearing his sheep, I collected all of my servants, herds and possessions, and with my two wives and children I stole away.

Laban pursued us and finally caught up with us near Mount Gilead (GIL ee-ad). There we met face-to-face. After a stormy beginning—when we both expressed freely our grievances to each other—we parted peaceably. As our caravan moved on, I became increasingly fearful since it was necessary for us to travel through the country of Edom, where my twin brother Esau had become a very powerful leader. After twenty years would he still be seeking my life in revenge for my earlier deceptions?

I called for several of my servants and gave instructions

to them that they must seek out my brother and humbly tell him that I wished to restore our friendship. Soon my messengers returned with the distressing news that Esau was advancing at full speed toward us with 400 armed men. That evening, while praying alone, I had another unusual spiritual experience. I felt that I wrestled all night with a heavenly being. As I clung to this person fiercely, he touched my hip socket and it became permanently wrenched. I told this angelic being that I would not let him go until he had first blessed me. He responded, "Your name will no longer be Jacob, but Israel, for as a prince you have power with God and with men, and have prevailed." When I awakened, I called the place Peniel (pe-NI-el), "because I saw God face to face and yet my life was spared."

As the early morning sun arose, I could see clearly my brother Esau with his 400 men coming toward me. To my great surprise, Esau threw his arms around my neck and embraced me. Together we wept joyfully. Later that day, we twin brothers parted as friends, Esau to his home in Seir (SEE-er) while I continued homeward to my father Isaac.

During this long journey, my loving wife Rachel gave birth to a second son, whom I called Benjamin—"the son of my right hand." Because of a difficult childbirth, however, my beloved wife died. I grieved deeply and buried her in a special tomb in Bethlehem. When we arrived home at last, how pleased I was to be with my dear father again just before he died.

In spite of my many faults and frailties, the Lord has blessed my life bountifully. It still amazes me that God would give me a vision of Himself there at Bethel and later even called me "a prince." I am overjoyed that from now on our chosen people will be known as "Israelites," after the new name given me at Peniel. May Jehovah ever be praised and His people worthy of His eternal blessing.

❋ ❋ ❋ ❋

Scripture References:
    Genesis 28:6–20; 29–35; Matthew 1:2; Luke 3:34; Acts 7:12; 14–15; 32; 46; Romans 9:11–13; 11:26; Hebrews 11:9, 20.

Spiritual Reflections:

Jacob's 12 sons by four different women became known as the twelve tribes of Israel:

- The sons of Leah: Reuben, Simeon, Levi, Judah, Issachar and Zebulun
- The sons of Rachel: Joseph and Benjamin
- The sons of Leah's maidservant: Gad and Asher
- The sons of Rachel's maidservant: Dan and Naphtali

Consider how a person with a flawed character such as Jacob's could be chosen as one of the three patriarchs of God's covenantal blessing to Israel.

Suggested Hymns:

- "We Are Climbing Jacob's Ladder"
- "O God, Our Help in Ages Past"

Joseph

The Lord was with Joseph and gave him success in
whatever he did (Genesis 39:23).

As I reflect upon a lifetime of unusual happenings—crushing
defeats as well as incredible triumphs—there is one
underlying truth that I have learned from all of these
experiences: God is in complete control of our lives, and
even in times of adversity, He is accomplishing His eternal
glory as well as our earthly good.

An early indication of this was when my ten older
stepbrothers conspired to have me killed. Instead they
sold me to a group of foreign merchants who took me to
Egypt. There they traded me off as a slave to Potiphar
(POT-i-fer), one of the high ranking officers of that land.
Now I can see clearly that even though my brothers
intended with these evil deeds to do me great harm, God
overruled for good.

Because I worked diligently in the Potiphar household, I
was promoted to the position of chief steward and given
complete control of all of his affairs. Again God allowed an
evil plot to overtake me. Potiphar's wife tried to seduce me,
but when I resisted her, she falsely accused me of making
sexual advances and had me put in prison, where I spent
the next two years. Once more, however, God used this
difficult experience to prepare me for even greater
responsibilities. In prison the Lord helped me interpret
correctly the dreams of two fellow prisoners who had
incurred the displeasure of Pharaoh, the ruler of the mighty
Egyptian empire. Some time later one of these prisoners, the
Pharaoh's butler, was restored to his royal position. One
day he overheard his monarch desperately plead for someone
to interpret his disturbing dream. When the court magicians
were not able to help, the butler told the king that in prison

he had known a young Hebrew who could interpret dreams accurately. The Pharaoh sent for me immediately.

With Jehovah's help, I not only interpreted the dream but was able to give important advice to the ruler. I foretold that after seven years of bountiful harvest in the land, there would be a grievous famine. I proposed a plan. If a portion of grain were stored during the seven plentiful years, it would be possible for everyone to survive during the ensuing lean years. The Pharaoh was so impressed with my plan that he immediately placed me in charge of carrying it out. I was honored with the title of governor and made second in command throughout the empire.

For the next seven years I worked diligently at this task. I traveled throughout Egypt to see where the richest harvests were to be found. In these areas I ordered storehouses built and made sure that the corn was stored carefully. In every city so much grain was stored that it soon became impossible to calculate the quantity. But at last the years of plenty ended. The dearth came to all the lands nearby; only in Egypt was there sufficient food. I ordered that the storehouses be opened for our people as well as for buyers from all the countries around Egypt.

One day I was told that from my homeland of Hebron (HE-bron) there was a delegation of Hebrew shepherds who wished to see me. I recognized them at once as my ten brothers; however, they did not know me and bowed before me with their faces to the ground. I spoke harshly to them as if I were a stranger, "Where do you come from?"

"From the land of Canaan, to buy food," they replied respectfully.

When I questioned them further, they told me that their youngest brother Benjamin was still at home with their elderly father Jacob. They also mentioned another brother who had been killed some years earlier. They spoke among themselves with great remorse about this incident, not realizing that I understood their Hebrew language. I was deeply moved to see my brothers again, especially to learn about my beloved father and younger brother, whom I loved dearly. In fact, I told them that they could not return for more food unless they brought Benjamin back with them.

After their donkeys were loaded, I sent home all except my brother Simeon (SIM-e-un), whom I kept as a ransom until Benjamin's return. Without their knowledge, I also gave a secret command to my servants that all the money these men had paid for the corn should be placed in the top of each sack. My brothers left, thankful for the corn, but much concerned about Simeon and what their father would say about Benjamin.

Several months later my brothers returned for another supply of food. This time Benjamin was with them. How my heart leaped with gladness when I saw him. I gave orders to my servants to prepare a special feast for these men at my house. My brothers were most fearful of this gesture, thinking that I was about to impose some further harshness upon them. When the meal was finished, however, their fears of me began to lessen.

Once again I sent them all home with their new supply of grain. This time in addition to returning their money in the sacks, I had my personal silver cup secretly placed in Benjamin's sack. Scarcely had my brothers reached the outskirts of the city than they discovered this. They returned to me, pleading their innocence with much remorse. At first I pretended to be very provoked, but I could keep quiet no longer. "I am Joseph," I cried. "I am your brother whom you sold into Egypt! God sent me here to save your lives. . . . Haste now, go to my father and tell him that his son Joseph is alive and that God has made him a ruler in Egypt. Tell him also that there is an area here in Egypt called Goshen where he can live and be near me. Tell him to bring his children, their families, the flocks and the herds and all that he has." I kissed each one tenderly and gave them special gifts for my father.

Before long I received word that my father, my brothers and their families—70 people in all—were arriving in Goshen. I left immediately in my chariot to meet them. My father and I wept over each other with unrestrained joy. He said that he was now ready to die after seeing his son whom he thought had long been dead. Our people settled down happily and prospered here in Goshen.

Now I know with certainty why God brought me to Egypt.

I am also beginning to understand the promise made to our Father Abraham by Jehovah God that He would one day develop a great nation from our Hebrew people. Truly God works in wondrous ways!

✽✽✽✽

Scripture References:
> Genesis 37; 39–45; 47; Hebrews 11:22

Spiritual Reflections:
> Consider personally how God often uses afflictions to accomplish His eternal glory and our earthly good.

Suggested Hymns:
- "God Moves in a Mysterious Way"
- "Be Still, My Soul"

Miriam

My servants will sing out of the joy of their hearts
(Isaiah 65:14).

My name means "bitterness" . . . and I often felt very angry
that our Jewish people were forced to suffer such cruel
oppression here in Egypt. For several centuries we had lived
in the land of Goshen under the harsh rule of this mighty
empire. Eventually the Egyptians grew fearful of our fast-
growing population and strength. They tried to keep us in
even greater bondage by making us work harder at
producing bricks for their many new building projects. Our
people became increasingly restless and discontent with their
grievous lives.

My mother and father were both descendants of Father
Abraham through Levi, Jacob's third son. Our family had
always been faithful worshipers of Jehovah, the one true God.
This was not easy since the Egyptians, with their heathen
worship of many gods, were hostile to our Hebrew faith and
practices. When my mother gave birth to a beautiful baby
boy, three-year-old Aaron and I, a teenager, were thrilled. We
were so happy with our precious new brother—until our joy
turned to great sorrow. The cruel Egyptian Pharaoh had issued
a decree that every newborn Jewish boy must be put to death
immediately. Mother was devastated, but since she was
determined to hide her baby son in our home, we lived in
constant fear that at any moment some Egyptian official would
discover him.

After a time my mother told me that God had given her a
plan for saving my baby brother's life. We made a papyrus
(pa-PI-rus) basket and covered it with tar in order that it
might float in the water. Together we journeyed to the banks
of the Nile River, where we placed my brother in the basket
among the reeds. Mother returned home while I stayed behind

and hid myself to keep a watchful eye on the little ark. When a group of young ladies appeared, I could tell that they were attending to the needs of an Egyptian royal princess as she enjoyed her morning bath. The princess was startled when she heard a faint cry from the basket floating nearby. Reaching to open the container, she exclaimed with amazement, "This beautiful child is one of the Hebrew babies!" As she gazed at him adoringly, I ran to her side and told her that I would be happy to find a Hebrew woman to care for her new-found child until he became older. I was pleased when she accepted my offer.

When I told her the news, Mother was overjoyed and cared for her young son tenderly. As he grew older, my parents earnestly taught him important truths about God and our Hebrew faith. Eventually mother took him to the Egyptian palace, where Pharaoh's daughter readily adopted him as her own son. The princess named him Moses, "drawn from the sea." My brother grew up as a prince in the royal court with the finest training possible and was highly respected among the leaders. Yet we heard that the Egyptian worship of pagan gods never satisfied him. Despite all of his cultural and educational background, Moses never forgot his early family training nor the sad plight of his fellow Hebrews in bondage.

One day we heard the thrilling news that Moses was coming to Goshen to see for himself the living conditions of our enslaved Jewish people. While there, he witnessed a typical case of an Egyptian officer physically abusing a Hebrew worker. Moses became so incensed at this injustice that he killed the Egyptian and hid his body in the sand. Soon, however, when the news of this deed was heard by Pharaoh, he demanded my brother's immediate death. Moses fled quickly to the land of Midian (MID-i-an) beyond the Egyptian border, where he remained for the next 40 years. During this time my brother Aaron and I continued to keep alive our people's faith in Jehovah God and their hope for deliverance from Egyptian bondage. Aaron served as a priest while I was known as a prophetess. We always believed that one day God would form a new nation from our people.

In time God revealed to Aaron that he should go into the desert to find our brother Moses. As they met, Moses related all that the Lord had told him about delivering the Hebrew people from their bondage. How thrilled I was to see my younger brother again and to learn of God's plans for using him to lead our people to the promised land. Aaron and I assured him that we would do all we could to assist him in accomplishing this mission.

Finally the day arrived when Moses and Aaron gave the orders for our departure from Egypt. We were to leave immediately that same night. Our people began the march toward the wilderness with great expectancy, joyous and confident in Jehovah. But our laughter changed to tears when we reached the great Red Sea. Before us were the mighty waters and behind us could be heard the sounds of Pharaoh's army, intent on destroying us. But Moses lifted his staff over the waters. Immediately the sea was swept back by a strong wind so our people could walk safely on dry land. As the Egyptian army tried to pursue us, Moses again raised his staff over the sea bed. The waters returned and totally destroyed our enemies!

When everyone was safely settled on dry ground, our people began praising God anew, realizing as never before the miracle-working power of our great Jehovah. They also had a new respect for Moses, God's anointed leader and deliverer. And right there Moses and I composed a song of gratitude to the Lord for freeing us from the Egyptian overlords, leading us safely through the Red Sea, and guiding us onward to the promised land. I gave tambourines to the women and led them in a joyous time of worship and celebration with these words of praise: "The Lord is my strength and my song; He has become my salvation. He is my God, and I will praise Him. . . . Sing to the Lord, for He is highly exalted. The horse and its rider He has hurled into the sea. Who among the gods is like You, O Lord? Who is like You—majestic in holiness . . . awesome in glory . . . working wonders? The Lord will reign forever and ever!"

✽ ✽ ✽ ✽

Scripture References:
Exodus 2; 15; 20:1; Hebrews 11:23

Spiritual Reflections:
Miriam was the first woman to be given the title of prophetess. Though little is mentioned of her in Scripture, Miriam is nevertheless a most important figure in the history of Israel. In addition to protecting her baby brother Moses, who later became Israel's greatest spiritual leader, Miriam shared in the political and spiritual development of the Jewish nation. Interestingly, the Bible (Mic. 6:4) equates her with Moses and Aaron when God later reminds the Hebrews of their heritage.

Suggested Hymns:
- "We Gather Together"
- "Joyful, Joyful, We Adore Thee"

Moses

The Lord spoke to Moses face to face as a man speaks
to his friend (Exodus 33: 11 NKJV).

As a prince in the palace of Pharaoh, I had always been
aware of my Hebrew heritage, even though I basked in the
opulence and ease of the royal Egyptian household. One
day I traveled to Goshen, where our Jewish people lived, to
see for myself how they were being treated. While there I
observed a Hebrew worker being cruelly mistreated by an
Egyptian overseer. Instantly my feeling for my own people
aroused in me such fury that I killed the abuser. When this
news reached the Egyptian capital, immediately I had to
escape to the land of Midian (MID-i-an) in the Sinai desert
beyond the Egyptian border. There I settled, began a family,
and remained for the next forty years.

I was peacefully tending my father-in-law's flock in the
wilderness near Mount Horeb (HO-reb) when suddenly I
saw a bush ablaze with fire, and from the bush I heard my
name:

> Moses, Moses! Do not come near here; remove the
> sandals from your feet, for the place on which you are
> standing is holy ground. I am the God of your father,
> the God of Abraham, the God of Isaac, and the God of
> Jacob. I have surely seen the affliction of My people
> who are in Egypt, so I have come down to deliver them
> from the Egyptians, and to bring them up from that
> land to a land flowing with milk and honey. Therefore,
> come now, and I will send you to Pharaoh, so that you
> may bring My people, the sons of Israel, out of Egypt.

In my fright I stammered, "But who am I, Lord, that I
should go to Pharaoh, and that I should bring the sons of

Israel out of Egypt? What would I say when my Hebrew
brethren began asking by what authority I had come?"

God reassured me. "Thus you shall say to the sons of
Israel, 'I AM has sent me. The Lord, the God of your fathers,
has sent me to you.'"

"But, Lord, I am so unskilled in my speaking. I have
always been a person with heavy speech and a slow tongue."

"Who has made man's mouth? Is it not I, the Lord? Now
then go, and I, even I, will be with your mouth, and teach you
what you are to say. There is also your older brother Aaron,
the Levite. I know that he speaks fluently. You can speak to
him and put the words in his mouth; and I, even I, will be
with your mouth and his mouth, and I will teach you what
you are to do."

With apprehension, I began the long journey to Egypt
and met my brother Aaron on the way. I told him all that
God had spoken at the burning bush. Arriving in Egypt, we
assembled the elders of Israel and told them of God's promise
of deliverance from their Egyptian bondage. The people
believed our words, accepted my leadership, and began to
worship the God of their fathers.

At the royal palace Aaron and I boldly confronted the
Egyptian Pharaoh. "Let the sons of Israel leave for a three
day journey into the wilderness to worship and sacrifice to
the God of their fathers." When Pharaoh refused, God sent
dreadful plagues, ending in the death of every first-born
except those whose doorposts were sprinkled with blood as
God had commanded. Shaken by this, Pharaoh relented. Our
people marched at once toward the wilderness. Approaching
the Red Sea, however, we were terrified when we heard
Pharaoh's army advancing upon us. But God swept back
the sea by a mighty wind so we could safely walk through!
Then we watched in amazement as the waters were hurled
back again to cover the entire Egyptian army. I led the people
in praise and gratitude to our great Jehovah.

But my struggles to get our people out of Egypt were
small compared with the task of leading them to the
promised land. There was grumbling about every difficulty
and a lack of appreciation for Jehovah's guidance and
provision of daily food. Often I heard: "Would to God we

had died in Egypt. In Egypt we sat by the flesh pots and ate bread to the full. And now Moses has brought us forth in this wilderness to kill the whole assembly with hunger."

Then came one of the saddest days of my life! Joshua and I had spent forty days with God on Mount Sinai, receiving the ordinances and commandments by which our people were to live and worship Him. As we approached the camp, we were horrified to see the people dancing and worshiping a golden calf that they had persuaded Aaron to make for them. I seized the calf, melted it in a fire, threw the powder upon the water, and made the people drink it!

On the mountain God also had given me a detailed plan for a beautiful Tent of Meeting where Israel could worship Him. The people began bringing their finest possessions to be used in the building of this portable tabernacle. It was truly a place of unusual beauty, worthy of the worship of our great God.

At last we approached the promised land! I chose twelve men, one leader from each tribe, to survey the entire countryside and bring back a complete report. After forty days they returned. The men were glowing in their accounts, but with the exception of Joshua and Caleb, all felt that it would be impossible for us to defeat the inhabitants there. Jehovah was so displeased with this lack of faith that He decreed that only Joshua and Caleb and the children of the current generation would ever be allowed to enter the promised land. We must wander for another forty years in the wilderness until all of the older generation had died.

The ensuing years of wandering were filled with more rebellion and discontent. Even my sister Miriam and brother Aaron, who had always been so faithful, turned against me and rivaled my leadership. Still I loved them both dearly and forgave them of their sin. It was a mournful period for all of Israel when we buried these precious loved ones with great honor.

On another occasion, when there was a shortage of water, the people again displayed a defiant spirit. After I prayed to God, He told me to take my staff and speak to a nearby rock to obtain water. By this time I had become greatly impatient with those rebellious people. Instead of speaking to the rock, I struck it angrily with my staff and spoke harshly to the people. Water gushed out but immediately I knew that I had dishonored Jehovah by my hasty temper and disobedience. Although God forgave me, He told me that because of my action, I would never be allowed to lead our people into the promised land.

I am now 120 years old, and though I am still strong and have clear eyesight, the time has come for laying down my leadership. God has told me to choose my faithful helper Joshua to be my successor. Jehovah has assured me, however, that before he takes me to my eternal home, He will allow me to view the promised land from the heights of Mount Nebo (NE-bo). What a thrill that will be! How gracious the Lord has been, in spite of my humble talents and many weaknesses, to use me as His spokesman and the deliverer of His people from Egypt.

Before departing on my journey to Mount Nebo, I will give our people my final blessing and this word of instruction: "Behold, I set before you this day a blessing and a curse. A blessing if you obey the Lord your God and a curse if you will not obey His commandments. . . . Take to heart all the words I have solemnly declared to you this day. . . . They are not just idle words for you. . . . They are your life!"

****

Scripture References:
>Exodus 2:1–25; 3:4; 5–25; Numbers 12:27; Deuteronomy 11:26–28; 32:46; 34; Hebrews 11:24–29

Spiritual Reflections:
>Moses was the preeminent figure in the Old Testament. He is mentioned in the New Testament more than any other Old Testament figure. His life divides into three forty year periods:
>• Forty years as an Egyptian prince
>• Forty years as an unassuming shepherd in the land of Midian
>• Forty years as a leader of the Israelites

Consider how the first eighty years prepared Moses for his important leadership role. Also, recall Jesus' thirty years of relative obscurity before beginnning His three year public ministry.

Suggested Hymns:
- "Guide Me, O Thou Great Jehovah"
- "God Leads Us Along"

Drama 9

Joshua

The God of Israel gives power and strength to His
people. Praise be to God! (Psalm 68:35).

I never thought of myself as a natural leader of people. In
fact, I have always been very aware of my own inadequacies
and weaknesses. While we were in Egyptian bondage and
during the years of wandering in the wilderness, I was
content simply to be a faithful helper to Moses . . . our
esteemed spiritual leader and deliverer.

I will never forget the day when Moses announced that
he would no longer be able to lead our people into the
promised land. He summoned me, laid his hand of blessing
on my head, and proclaimed publicly that I was to be the
new leader. Once the land was possessed, I was to divide it
among the twelve tribes as their inheritance. After Moses'
death, the responsibility for accomplishing these tasks
seemed overwhelming. But then I heard the voice of
Almighty God speaking to me: "Be strong and courageous,
Joshua, for you will bring the Israelites into the land I
promised them on oath, and I myself will be with you. I will
give you every place where you set your foot. . . . No one
will be able to stand up against you all the days of your life.
As I was with Moses, so I will be with you. I will never
leave you nor forsake you."

With the assurance of my call from God and with this
promise of His presence, I was renewed in strength and
vigor and felt ready to lead. I ordered the officers of the
people to go through the camp, telling everyone to get their
supplies together in preparation for conquering the land
promised to our forefathers by Jehovah.

I knew that the most important city in Canaan was Jericho.
We would need to possess it as a stronghold for launching
further attacks throughout the land. I sent two spies to survey

the city before beginning our advance. After several days they returned with the report that the Canaanites were already fearful of us. Since our men felt we could surely take Jericho, I gave the order for our people to begin their march. When we reached the Jordan River, we camped there for three days. As the time to cross the river approached, I instructed everyone to keep their eyes on the Ark of the Covenant and to follow the priests who carried it. I also urged our people to consecrate themselves anew to the Lord and to be grateful for the amazing things He was about to do for us. We began our advance into the river. No sooner had the priests' feet touched the water's edge than the mighty flood waters from upstream stopped flowing, and the waters moving southward toward the Dead Sea were completely cut off. Every person was able to cross over safely on dry ground!

The Lord told me to have one man from each of the twelve tribes take a stone from the river's bed and prepare a memorial. It would be a constant reminder of what God had done for us that day and our need to trust Him in the days ahead. We established a bridgehead at Gilgal and built our stone memorial to God's faithfulness.

At this time the Lord God revealed to me that our people were to walk around the walled city of Jericho for six days. We were to follow the priests as they played their horns in front of the Ark of the Covenant. On the seventh day we were to march seven times around the city. Though our tactics no doubt seemed foolish to many, we did exactly as God had commanded. On the seventh march there was a blast from the trumpets and a shout from the people. The walls fell with a mighty crash and all within were annihilated! Once again our God had been true to His word.

In the more than twenty years that followed our entry into Canaan, there have been many more battles fought and enemies subdued as we sought to possess this entire land for God. There have been times when our people turned away from Jehovah, forsook His commandments, and followed after pagan gods. Yet the Lord has always remained merciful, faithful and forgiving.

But the responsibilities of leadership and the passing of

years have made me feel old and tired. I have tried to impress upon our people that after I am gone, they must continue to serve God and obey His commands. I have told them that each person must choose either a life of rebelling or a life of blessing. It is my fervent prayer that they will follow with conviction the choice I have often declared, "But as for me and my household, we will serve the Lord!"

✻✻✻✻

Scripture References:

Exodus 17:9; Numbers 13:8; Deuteronomy 31:23; Hebrews 11:30; the book of Joshua, written about the fourteenth century B.C.

Spiritual Reflections:

Joshua is a model of faithful obedience to the Lord's commands. Many Bible scholars also see him as a type of Christ, who, like Joshua, is leading His people into their promised land, heaven.

Suggested Hymns:
- "A Charge to Keep I Have"
- "Faith Is the Victory"

Rahab

By faith the prostitute Rahab . . . was not killed with
those who were disobedient (Hebrews 11:31).

My life in the famous city of Jericho was not one to be
envied, but it was all I had ever known. For a number of
years I lived in a most unusual home. It was located on top
of the walls of Jericho. Actually our fortified city had a double
wall encircling it, and my house was built over the gap
between the walls. My home was well known to all,
especially to the officials of our city as well as to the many
prosperous merchant travelers. They all knew me simply as
"Rahab the Harlot."

Ours was the most powerful and thriving city in the
entire land of Canaan. It was also a beautiful place, widely
known as the "Place of Palms and Fragrance." Yet in spite
of all this prosperity and beauty about me, I felt an
emptiness in my life. Somehow our lewd and sensuous
worship of Baal and the goddess Ashtoreth (ASH-to-reth)
had never been spiritually satisfying to me. Recently some
of our traveling visitors related accounts about the Israelites
and said that these religious people were now encamped
just across the Jordan River. They told thrilling stories about
the Israelite's God and the unusual miracles He had done
for them since they first fled from Egypt more than forty
years ago. I had a growing hunger to learn more about this
powerful Deity.

One day two Jewish strangers visited me in my home. I
did not think this odd until I realized that they had not
come for the usual favors. Instead they began to tell me
about their great Jehovah God and how He would soon
deliver our city of Jericho into their hands. My curiosity was
aroused. It wasn't long, however, before our chief ruler sent
several officials to my home with this message: "Bring out

the men who came to you and entered your house . . . because they have come to spy out the whole land."

Somehow I had the feeling that these two Jews were good men and that I should protect them. Instead of producing the strangers, I quickly hid them under some stalks of flax which were drying on the roof. Then I told the king's officers, "Yes, the men came to me, but I did not know from where they had come. At dusk, when it was time to close the city gate, the men left. Go after them quickly. You may still catch up with them."

I returned to the two men hiding on the roof. After feeding them an evening meal, I began to question them further about their Jewish religion. I was anxious to learn more about their Jehovah God. Gradually I began to realize that this was the truth for which my heart had been searching. With heartfelt conviction I told them, "I truly believe that the Lord your God is God in heaven above and on the earth below and will give this land to the Israelites."

My only concern now was for the safety of my parents and family. "Give me a sure sign that you will spare the lives of my father and mother, my brothers and sisters, and all who belong to them," I pleaded. The two Jewish men assured me that if I followed their directions, my life and the lives of my entire household would be saved during their victorious return.

Still later that evening we planned their escape. I bound a scarlet rope about the waist of one of the men and lowered him from my window to the ground below. After he was safely down, I did the same for the second man. Now they would not have to go out of the city gate and risk capture and certain death. Before they left I advised them that they could escape the pursuers by hiding for three days in the mountain west of Jericho before returning to their home camp. The two men told me that I must keep the scarlet rope hanging from my window in order to ensure the lives of my family.

A week later we heard frightening reports that the Israelites had crossed the Jordan River miraculously over dry ground and were now marching toward our city. Then something strange began to occur. For the next six days, while we remained shut up within our walls, the Israelites marched around our city once each day. They blew rams' horns and followed a strange looking box with two golden cherubims stretched across its lid. Though fearful, our people were much amused at this humorous spectacle and jeered at the crowd as they passed. The seventh day came, with the Israelites still marching and blowing. On their seventh time around, suddenly a tremendous shout was heard. Our mighty walls collapsed with a deafening crash! Instantly the Israelite army poured into the city with drawn swords and destroyed every living thing in sight. When the army approached my home, we were terrified! But the same two men whom I had let down through the window came in and escorted my family and me to a place of safety. From that entire city, we were the only survivors.

I continued my new life with these Hebrew people and began to worship their Jehovah God as my own Lord. I married one of their leaders, a man named Salmon (SAL-mon), and now God has blessed our happy home with a son we called Boaz (BO-az).

How I praise Jehovah, the one true God, for sparing my life and changing me from a sinful harlot to one of His own dear people.

****

Scripture References:
    Joshua 2; 6:25; Hebrews 11:31; James 2:25

Spiritual Reflections:
    Rahab was the great-great grandmother of David the king and an ancestress of Mary, the mother of Jesus. Boaz became the husband of Ruth, and they were the parents of Obed, father of Jesse, father of King David and the forerunner of Jesus Christ, the Messiah.

Suggested Hymns:
    • "Only a Sinner"
    • "Depth of Mercy"

Drama 11

Caleb

Blessed are those whose strength is in You . . . they go from strength to strength (Psalm 84:5, 7).

Although I am now eighty-five years of age, I feel as vigorous as I did forty-five years ago when Moses chose me with Joshua and ten other tribal leaders to spy out Canaan. This was the land that Jehovah God had promised us when He led us out of our bondage in Egypt. All that remained was the defeating of the enemies and the possessing of our national inheritance.

For forty days we twelve men searched and surveyed the region secretly. And what a land it was! The entire countryside seemed fertile and productive. Never before had we seen foliage and fruit growing as it did there. On one occasion we cut a single cluster of grapes and it took two of us to carry it on a pole between us. It was a thrill to see and enjoy this beautiful place. But there were also some very real problems. The cities were all walled and heavily fortified, and the people seemed unusually large and impressive. In fact, we felt so small and inadequate—much like grasshoppers—when compared to them.

Returning to our people in the wilderness, we showed them some of the unusual fruit that we brought back with us and told them about the richness and beauty of the land. Joshua and I reported that we should take possession of this land, for we could overcome it with God's help. The other ten leaders insisted that it would be impossible for us ever to defeat the enemies, who were like mighty giants, living in large fortified cities and devouring all those who opposed them.

Our people panicked with fear. I tried to calm them with a reminder of Jehovah's presence and guidance, but they murmured and cried throughout an entire night. Then they began to grumble and complain against our leaders, Moses and Aaron. Hysterically they cried, "Why is the Lord bringing us into this land to fall by the sword? Our wives and children will be taken as plunder. Let us appoint new leaders and return to Egypt."

Crushed by the rebelliousness of the people, Moses and Aaron fell on their faces in the presence of the assembly. Joshua and I were also deeply troubled, tearing our garments in distress. We addressed the people and reminded them again that with God's help we could surely possess this good land. "Only do not rebel against the Lord and do not fear the people. The Lord is with us," we pleaded. But our people refused to listen to us, shouting that they wanted us stoned!

Then the Lord spoke to Moses and Aaron. "How long shall I bear with this evil congregation who are grumbling against me? How long will they not believe in Me, despite all the signs which I have performed in their midst?" Because of their unbelief God pronounced a sentence of death upon every adult of that generation. Only their children, as well as Joshua and I, would ever see the promised land. All others would die in the wilderness. When the people heard this pronouncement, they wept bitterly.

I never forgot the special blessing given to me by Jehovah God Himself.

> My servant Caleb, because he had a different spirit and has followed me fully, I will bring him into the land which he entered, and his descendants shall take possession of it.

This promise has been a source of strength each day, knowing that what God said, He would surely do. Now after forty-five years we have entered our promised land. The once mighty city of Jericho, which God miraculously gave us, has been our stronghold in our conquest of the enemies in this entire region. There was still one special mountain, Mount Hebron (HE-bron), which I had always cherished. It was here many years ago that God first spoke to our father Abraham when He promised this land of

Canaan to His chosen people. Recently I reminded Joshua, our appointed leader after Moses' death, that before Moses died he promised this mountain to me as my family inheritance. Joshua graciously consented and gave me his blessing. Soon the mighty enemies on Mount Hebron were defeated. Jehovah once again was true to His eternal word!

✳ ✳ ✳ ✳

Scripture References:
    Numbers 13:6; 14:3–4, 9, 11, 24, 27; Joshua 14

Spiritual Reflections:
    "God wants us to be victors, not victims; to grow, not grovel; to soar, not sink; to overcome, not be overwhelmed."

—William H. Ward

Suggested Hymns:
* "O for a Faith That Will Not Shrink"
* "Soldiers of Christ, Arise"

Deborah

The horse is made ready for the day of battle, but the victory rests with the Lord (Proverbs 21:31).

I have been anointed by God to be a judge in Israel. I am called the "Bee" for that is what my name Deborah means . . . and I can be a sting for my enemies . . . but honey for my friends. Each day I wait here under my palm tree for the people to come up into the hills from Ramah (RA-mah) and Bethel (BETH-el) to counsel with me. My heart is often heavy for them with their many problems, disappointments, and petty quarrels. I would not be equal to the great task God has placed before me without His constant guidance. Sometimes I compose songs and poetry to comfort my people. The Lord gives me strength and wisdom for my decisions . . . and at times He speaks to me in clear commands, as He did not long ago!

For many years there had been peace in Israel. But the people did evil continually until at last God sent—without warning—the mighty army of Jabin (JA-bin), King of Canaan. With nine hundred chariots of iron they destroyed our vineyards, abused our women, captured and killed our children . . . for twenty years! The people felt helpless and forsaken. Many times I tried to persuade them to cast themselves upon God's mercy and drive out the Canaanites boldly, but they were too fearful! So the land of Israel grew darker every year.

But at last God's voice was heard . . . and by me, His lowly servant. The message was to call Barak (BAR-ak), the commander of our army, and tell him to gather ten thousand men and lead them to steep Mount Tabor (TA-ber) near Nazareth. As soon as the enemy approached, the Israelites were to climb the mountain quickly to attack from above! God promised complete victory for His people.

Barak was astonished at the message, and fearful! What could his small band of poorly equipped men do, on foot and with little ammunition, against the iron chariots of General Sisera (SIS-er-ah)? He turned to me: "I will obey the command, Deborah, only if you will go with us into battle!"

I, a woman, lead an army of men? . . . leaving my husband and my dear people? But then the sustaining presence of Almighty God seemed to surround me. "I will surely go, Barak. Lead the way!"

We marched to the base of steep Mount Tabor. There stood the powerful army of Sisera, ready for battle! "Up, Barak," I shouted, "up the mountain with your army, for this is the day the Lord will give Sisera into your hand! Does not the Lord Himself go before you to fight for you? Up, Barak!"

As the men of Israel scrambled to higher levels, lightning began to flash. Then thunder roared as a fearful storm swept down before the advancing army of Canaan! Their frightened horses ran wild! Their chariots were thrown into confusion on the steep muddy slopes! Terror seized the enemy as they saw the waters of the nearby river rising in wild force! It was the hand of God. Instantly the Israelites swooped down upon the Canaanites with a triumphant cry of victory, driving them into the sea below. The dreadful army of Sisera was destroyed! It was truly a miracle.

On that day I offered this song of victorious praise to God:

> I will sing to the Lord, I will sing.
> I will make music to the Lord, the God of Israel.
> Village life in Israel ceased, until I , Deborah, arose
> . . . a mother in Israel.
> From the heavens the stars fought, from their
> courses they fought against Sisera.
> The river Kishon (KI-shon) swept them away.
> March on, my soul, be strong! So may all Your
> enemies perish, O Lord!
> But may they who love You be like the sun when it
> rises in its strength.

* * * *

Scripture References:
    Judges 4 and 5

Spiritual Reflections:
    The book of Judges, written in the eleventh century
    B.C., is the record of the activities of twelve men and one
    woman (Deborah) who served as judges in Israel after
    Joshua's death. Deborah was recognized as a prophetess
    as well.

Suggested Hymns:
    • "A Mighty Fortress"
    • "Lead On, O King Eternal"

Drama 13

Gideon

The battle is not yours, but God's (2 Chronicles 20:15).

How privileged I feel to have been a judge in Israel for the past forty years. God chose me, a humble farmer, to help our people settle their many disputes and problems. I also urged them to maintain their worship of Jehovah and to follow after His commands. During these years the Israelites have enjoyed the Lord's blessing and have lived in peace with their many pagan neighbors. The grateful people recently prevailed upon me to be their king, but I have told them that neither I nor my son will ever rule over them. The Lord Himself must be their ruler.

Our nation has not always enjoyed peace and prosperity. When I was a young man, we were overrun by the Midianites (MID-i-an-ites), a wild, uncultured people, who took great delight in robbing and harassing others. For seven long years they made life miserable for us. They plundered our crops and cattle and left us with little substance. The only way our Jewish people survived at all was to live and hide in the caves of the mountains.

Finally, in desperation, our people cried out to Jehovah . . . whom they had been despising with their idol worship. And though I was young, the spiritual condition of our people had greatly disturbed me. One day I was busily threshing wheat and pondering these matters. Suddenly an angel of the Lord appeared, startling me with the announcement, "Jehovah is with you, Gideon, mighty warrior."

I, a man of valor? Was this angel mocking me? I felt so cowardly hiding from our enemies here in the vineyard. "Oh, my Lord," I replied, "if Jehovah is with us, why has all this happened to us? Where are all His wonders that our fathers told us about when they said, 'Did not the Lord bring us out of Egypt?' But now the Lord has abandoned us and put us into the hands of the Midianites."

The angelic messenger commanded, "Go in the strength you have and save Israel out of Midian's hand. Am I not sending you?"

I was shaken, and fearful of the task given me. Several times I pleaded with Jehovah to prove His presence with me by special signs. On one occasion I prayed, "If You will save Israel by my hand as You have promised—look, I will place a wool fleece on the threshing floor. In the morning if there is dew only on the fleece and all the ground is dry, then I will know that You will save Israel by my hand . . . as You said."

Early the next morning I rose up and pressed the fleece together. A bowl of water poured out. Yet hesitantly I prayed again to God. "Do not be angry with me. Allow me one more test with the fleece. This time make the fleece dry and the ground covered with dew." In the morning I went nervously to look. All the ground was covered with dew—only the fleece was dry!

Immediately I sent out a call to the various tribes for volunteer warriors for our army. I was proud of the mighty host of 32,000 men who responded. I felt certain now that Jehovah was surely with us. How surprised I was when the Lord told me that it was too large an army and that I should dismiss any who were fearful. As 22,000 men returned to their homes, I was left with an army of 10,000 warriors. But again the Lord told me that there were still too many. "Take them down to the water and I will sift them for you there." As I led the men to the water, the Lord directed, "Separate those who lap the water with their tongues like a dog from those who kneel down to drink." To my dismay only three hundred men lapped with their hands to their mouths. Then the Lord said, "With these three-hundred men that lapped I will save you and give the Midianites into your hands."

We prepared for battle! I divided the three-hundred men into three companies and placed trumpets and empty jars with torches in the hands of each man. "Watch me," I told them. "Follow my lead. When I get to the edge of the enemy camp, do exactly as I do. When our trumpets are blown, blow yours and shout, 'For the Lord and for Gideon.'"

As soon as the Midianites had changed their guards, we attacked! We surrounded their camp and the men blew and shouted together! In wild hysteria the Midianites scattered and began to kill each other with their own swords. Soon their entire army was in complete disarray as they fled frantically. My messengers raced throughout the countryside to tell our people to pursue them, and the mighty Midianite army was totally destroyed. Once again Jehovah God had been faithful to His chosen people with a complete victory over our dreaded enemy.

Truly God is good. He has blessed me with a long life of service for Him and the joy of a large family. There were many times when I failed to trust Him as I should. Yet He has always been patient and kind. I humbly give Him all the glory!

* * * *

Scripture References:
    Judges 6–7; Hebrews 11:32

Spiritual Reflections:
    Gideon was the fifth recorded judge of Israel and was considered by many to be one of the greatest of them all.

> Little is much, when God is in it!
>   Labor not for wealth or fame;
> There's a crown—and you can win it,
>   if you'll go in Jesus' name.
>   —Littie J. Suffield

Suggested Hymns:
    • "Onward, Christian Soldiers"
    • "Savior, Like a Shepherd Lead Us"

Delilah

My son, if sinners entice you, do not give in to them
(Proverbs 1:10).

Here in the Valley of Sorek (SO-rek) in the land of the
Philistines, my friends call me Delilah (De-LI-lah), the dainty
one. Throughout my lifetime I have learned to use my natural
beauty and charm to lure the interests of many men.

Our Philistine people have become strong and prosperous.
Our farms have produced rich harvests and the cities have
become mighty. Our land is adjacent to Canaan, where the
Jews live, but we no longer fear them or their God Jehovah.
In fact, we have begun to disdain them as if they were slaves
and often rob their crops and take their best farms. The only
person who ever challenged us was one of their leaders
whom they called a judge—a mighty man named Samson.
He was a giant of a person with superhuman strength. His
greatest delight seemed to be to get even with us, and he
was constantly taunting us with his extraordinary feats. Can
you believe that on one occasion he single-handedly snared
three-hundred foxes, tied them tail to tail, put a lighted torch
between each pair, and set them loose in our harvest lands?
They burned up the grain and destroyed our vineyards and
olive plantations.

How surprised and pleased I was one day when this
mighty Samson visited our valley. He noticed me and before
long was expressing strong interest and even deep affection
for me. Soon our Philistine leaders heard the rumor that
this dreaded enemy was visiting me on a regular basis.
They offered me a fortune if I could succeed in learning
the secret of this man's superior strength so that he might
be subdued and made their prisoner.

I had become very fond of Samson . . . but the lure of this
large sum of money moved me to betray him. On three

different occasions I did my best to seduce this Israelite giant, but each time he embarrassed me just when it seemed that he had been trapped. When he came back for still another visit, I pouted and produced many tears as I sobbed, "Samson, you don't really love me. If you did, you would hide nothing from me. You would tell me all that is in your heart, and let me know the secret of your strength."

He could resist me no longer. Reluctantly he confided that he was a Nazarite and that if his hair were once shaven, he would be like any ordinary man. Later, when he became drowsy, I put his head gently on my lap. While he slept soundly I called for my servant, who quickly sheared off all of his golden hair. Then I shouted, "Samson, wake up, the Philistines are upon thee!" As the Philistine leaders came rushing in, Samson did not realize that the Lord Jehovah was no longer with him. His superhuman strength was truly gone and he proved no match for these men. Easily they bound him, carried him in triumph to the prison, cruelly burned out his eyes, and forced him to grind corn like an animal with the other slaves in the prison. Our mighty enemy had fallen!

Some time later our Philistine people assembled for a special festival in the temple of Dagon (DA-gon), one of our gods. We were celebrating our conquest of the Jews and especially of their champion, the mighty Samson. Soon the people began shouting, "Our god Dagon has delivered Samson into our hands. Now let the slave come out here and entertain us."

The suggestion was greeted with wild raucous cheering! A small boy led Samson to the center court and placed him between the two supporting columns. His golden hair had once again grown to its full length. What an impressive sight he made as he stood there before the three thousand shouting Philistines. We saw him speak to the lad who held his hand. Those nearby heard him say, "Put me where I can feel the pillars that support the temple, so that I may lean against them." With his huge hands resting against the massive pillars, he could be heard praying aloud to his God, "O Sovereign Lord, remember me. . . . Please strengthen me just once more and let me with one blow get revenge on the Philistines for my two eyes. . . . Let me die with these people!"

Silently Samson pressed his hands against the pillars, and as he pushed with all his strength, the temple crashed on the mass of people! Amazingly, he killed more Philistines with his death than he did even during his lifetime.

Samson's final prayer had been answered.

✳ ✳ ✳ ✳

Scripture References:
> Judges 16; Hebrews 11:32

Spiritual Reflections:
> Samson was the last of the Spirit-led judges of Israel before Samuel. He was born about 1090 B.C. at the beginning of the forty-year-long Philistine oppression of the Jews. The people had become so disheartened that during Samson's twenty-year ministry there was no national repentance or desire for a deliverer. Perhaps this accounts in part for Samson's moral weakness even though he was in most ways a God-fearing leader.

Suggested Hymns:
> • "Yield Not to Temptation"
> • "My Soul, Be on Your Guard"

Drama 15

Ruth

Then you will know that I the Lord am your Savior (Isaiah 60:16).

Growing up in the land of Moab, I had no idea of the changes that would come to me in later years or the foreign country that would be my final home. In our Moabite town was a Hebrew family from the city of Bethlehem in Judah. They had come to our region to escape a severe famine in their homeland. I became interested in them because of their unusual religion . . . the faithful worship of Israel's God, Jehovah. Our people are descendants of Father Lot, and we have always worshiped the ancient god Chemosh (KE-mosh).

The Jewish man, Elimelech (e-LIM e-lek), had a gracious wife named Naomi (NA-o-mi) and two very attractive sons about my own age. Before long my girlfriend Orpah (OR-pah) and I became friendly with these fine young men. When their father became ill and died, we were very saddened and became especially close to his wife as we tried to comfort her. Eventually, Orpah and I were married to the two sons and were very happy.

But then great sorrow entered our lives. Within a brief period both of our dear husbands died, leaving three lonely widows. In our country there was little opportunity for women without husbands or sons to care for them. It wasn't long before my mother-in-law Naomi announced that she was going to leave Moab and return to her own people in Bethlehem because there was no longer a famine there. She advised us to return to our parents' homes. Orpah and I were heartbroken at the thought of never seeing her again.

When the day for departure came, we both walked with Naomi for some distance. As we tearfully said our farewells, she reminded us that we must return to Moab as it would be impossible for us to survive in a strange land. She kissed us tenderly and wished God's blessing on us. Reluctantly Orpah turned to go back, but something kept me from following her. Earnestly I cried out, "Entreat me not to leave you or to turn back from you. Where you go I will go, and where you stay I will stay. Your people will be my people and your God my God. Where you die I will die, and there will I be buried. May the Lord deal with me, be it ever so severely, if anything but death separates you from me." Deeply moved by this, Naomi took my hand affectionately as we continued traveling. After several days we reached the gates of Bethlehem.

It seemed as if the whole town had heard that Naomi was returning home with her Moabite daughter-in-law. There was a great crowd to welcome us. Then I heard them whisper to one another, "Is this really Naomi, the lovely and pleasant maiden who married Elimelech? How sad and faded she has become since leaving us." Though life had treated her cruelly during the years in Moab, I always knew that her faith in Almighty God had never wavered.

We arrived in Bethlehem during the barley harvest season, a busy but joyous time for the people. I soon learned an interesting fact about the customs of the Jews and their concern for the poor. After the fields have been gleaned by the owner and his workers, anyone in need had the right to glean the fields a second time and keep the grain.

Since we were very poor, I said that I would go into the fields and gather food for ourselves in this way. Naomi told about her departed husband's well-to-do relative, Boaz (BO-az), who owned many of the surrounding fields. She suggested that I first find his lands and try working there.

I made my way to these fields and gleaned there with the many others who were trying to fill their sacks with grain. Soon a friendly, well-dressed, middle-aged man entered the field and greeted the reapers politely. "Jehovah be with you!"

"Jehovah bless you!" they replied.

Directing his gaze at me, Boaz asked his foreman, "Who is that yonder damsel?"

"She is Ruth, the fair maiden who came back with your relative Naomi from the land of Moab," he answered.

When the impressive man walked over to me, I was

frightened, for I expected that he would ask me to leave his field. But he spoke kindly, "My daughter, listen to me. Don't go and glean in another field. Stay here with my servant girls. I have told the men not to touch you, and whenever you are thirsty, take a drink from the water jars the men have filled."

I bowed low to the ground before asking, "Why have I found grace in your eyes, seeing I am just a stranger?"

"I have heard all that you did to help your dear mother-in-law. Jehovah recompense your work . . . and a full reward be given you of Jehovah, the God of Israel, under whose wings you have come to trust."

I hurried home to tell Naomi all that had happened. She cried out with much joy, "Blessed be he of the Lord, who has not left off his kindness to the living and the dead. . . . He is truly one of our kinsman-redeemers."

As I returned to work in those same fields each day, I could sense that Boaz was often watching me closely. Then one day as the harvest season was drawing to a close, my wise mother-in-law startled me with the announcement, "The time has come for you to ask Boaz to marry you." She explained that it was a normal custom in this land that if a man died and left his wife without a child, it was the responsibility of the nearest relative to marry the widow and maintain the continuity of the family name. Since Boaz was a relative and appeared fond of me, I agreed to pursue Naomi's advice.

Boaz said he loved me dearly and desired to marry me. But there was another even closer relative living in our city who had the first claim. After Boaz conferred with the city's ruling elders about this matter, this next of kin agreed before witnesses that he would stand aside and allow Boaz to marry me.

How happy our marriage was, since my husband was such an upright and kind man. We established a God-fearing home. Before long Jehovah blessed us with a son, whom we named Obed (O-bed). My dear mother-in-law was greatly comforted by this child in her old age. She cared for him as gently as though he were her very own son.

Somehow I sensed in my spirit that this child was destined

to be special. How good the God of Israel has been in leading me to this foreign land and caring for me as one of His chosen people.

****

Scripture Reference:
The book of Ruth, written in the eleventh century B.C.

Spiritual Reflections:
Obed was the father of Jesse, the father of King David, the forerunner of Jesus Christ. Ruth was one of the four women named by Matthew in the genealogy of Christ (Matt. 1:5–6).

Suggested Hymns:
- "O Love That Wilt Not Let Me Go"
- "Happy the Home When God Is There"

Drama 16

Hannah

All my longings lie open before You, O Lord (Psalm 38:9).

Year after year I had prayed fervently to be blessed with a child, but the Lord God did not grant my desire. I became depressed and sorrowful. Friends and family taunted me about my barrenness until I suffered such humiliation that at times I could scarcely eat my meals. I knew that my husband Elkanah (el-KA-nah) loved me dearly because he was always thoughtful and good to me, but I was still not a happy wife. He would ask, "Hannah, why are you weeping? Why don't you eat? Don't I mean more to you than ten sons?" But I could not be consoled.

I determined that when the proper time of the year came, I would go up to the temple at Shiloh (SHI-lo) to worship and sacrifice. There I would earnestly petition God once again to send us a child. Surely in such a sacred place my prayers would be heard, I thought.

When we arrived at the holy temple, I was filled with awe and anticipation. I wanted to be alone to pray, so I drew aside to a secluded spot. As I stood looking up to God, my grief was so overwhelming that the tears flowed freely. Silently I pleaded, "O Lord Almighty, if You will only look upon Your servant's misery and give her a son . . . then I will give him to the Lord for all the days of his life, and no razor will ever be used on his head."

Although I had not noticed, Eli the priest was passing nearby. As I continued to pray, I was so engrossed that my lips were moving as I silently made my vow to God. Eli saw this as he stopped to watch and was certain that I had become drunk and was babbling to myself. Angrily he approached me, calling out loudly, "How long will you keep on getting drunk? Get rid of your wine!"

I was startled by his harsh voice and upset by his misunderstanding. Sinking to my knees before him, I protested, "Not so, my lord. I am a woman who is deeply troubled. I have not been drinking strong drink. . . . I was pouring out my soul to the Lord. Do not take your servant for a wicked woman; I have been praying here out of my great anguish and grief." And my tears continued to cover my uplifted face.

For a hushed moment Eli continued looking at me. Then his expression changed from rebuke and disapproval to kindness and understanding. He seemed to pause while listening to an inner voice . . . then he helped me to my feet. "Go in peace," he said softly, "and may the God of Israel grant you what you have asked of Him."

At once my soul was filled with a quiet calm. I answered him, "May thy servant find favor in your eyes." Wiping my tear-stained face, I went serenely to the place where my husband and friends were gathered for a meal. My fears and sadness were now gone. With contentment and composure I returned with my husband to our home in Ramah (RA-mah).

And the Lord God remembered me. Not long after this, my precious son was born! I gave him the name Samuel, meaning "I have asked the Lord for him." What joy he brought to our lives and how tenderly I cared for him. I did not go to the temple again until Samuel was old enough to be presented there. Then we brought him to the house of the Lord at Shiloh to fulfill that vow I had made. When Eli approached us I exclaimed, "Oh, my lord, I am the woman who stood here beside you praying for this child. God has granted me what I asked of Him. Now I give him to the Lord for his entire life." I offered these words of grateful praise: "My heart rejoices in the Lord. There is no rock like our God . . . for the foundations of the earth are the Lord's . . . upon them He has set the world. He will guard the feet of His saints, but the wicked will be silenced in darkness."

Little Samuel began to minister before the Lord and assisted Eli in the care of the temple. Each year when we went up to Shiloh for the annual sacrifice, I brought my son a new robe to wear. How my heart rejoiced as he continued to grow not only physically but also in favor with the Lord and with the people. As he developed, it became evident that the Lord was with him in a very special way. And Jehovah God did not forget the presentation of my son for the Lord's service . . . for to take Samuel's place in our home, three fine sons and two lovely daughters were given to us.

How faithful is Almighty God to all who place their trust in Him!

✳ ✳ ✳ ✳

Scripture References:
    1 Samuel 1; 2:1–11

Spiritual Reflections:
    Compare Hannah's expression of praise with Mary's Magnificat (Luke 1:46–55).

Suggested Hymns:
    • "Have Thine Own Way, Lord"
    • "Take My Life and Let It Be"

Samuel

Speak, for your servant is listening (1 Samuel 3:10).

I really did not know our Jehovah God personally until one night, when I was a young boy, He came and stood near my bedside and awakened me with His voice. I was astonished that the Almighty would speak directly to me, a child, but I knew that I must listen carefully and obey His words. I was aware that even before I was born, my mother had dedicated me to be a Nazarite (NAZ-i-rite), giving lifelong service to the Lord. When I was brought to the sanctuary here at Shiloh (SHI-lo) at an early age, I was grateful that I could assist Eli, the aged priest, in his daily duties. But after God spoke with me, I realized His presence more each day and knew with certainty that He had destined me to serve Him in a special way.

My instructions from the Lord that night were to tell the priest that divine judgment would soon fall upon his household. Eli's sons had done evil by living immoral lives and by stealing from the temple the meat intended for the sacrifices. Eli had never corrected them for this. I was reluctant to deliver the message but realized that I must obey God. I was surprised at Eli's humble response, "He is the Lord. . . . Let Him do what is good in His eyes." Several years later when the Philistines attacked Israel and captured the Ark of the Covenant, Eli's two sons were killed in battle. When Eli heard the tragic news about the Ark and the death of his sons, he tumbled off his chair and died.

As I was growing up, God continued to reveal Himself to me. While leading the worship services at Shiloh, I would listen attentively for His voice. He gave words of instruction to me for the people, and before long the entire nation of Israel recognized that I was truly a prophet of the Lord. They called me "the Seer" and said, "He is the one who can see God and tell us what is in our hearts." I was also appointed by Jehovah to be a judge over the people. Each year I made a tour of the cities to listen to disputes and problems, and after interceding with the Lord for the people, I delivered my judgments to them.

Following a war with our enemy, the Philistines, and their capture of the Ark of the Covenant, the Israelites felt sad and defeated. They realized that the glory of the Lord had departed from them. After another twenty years had passed, in deep mourning they began to seek fervently for deliverance from the oppression of this enemy. When the people entreated me, I directed them to gather the entire nation at a place called Mizpah (MIZ-pah). Here they must first repent of their idolatrous worship and confess their sins to Almighty God. After they had done this, I interceded for them with the Lord.

When the enemy heard that the Israelites had all gathered in one place, they planned their attack. Our fearful people pleaded frantically with me, "Do not stop crying out to the Lord our God for us that He may save us from the hand of the Philistines!" I first took a suckling lamb and offered it as a burnt offering to Jehovah. Then I prayed earnestly that He would rescue His people.

The mighty Philistines began their vicious assault . . . but God's answer came quickly. There was a roar of loud crashing thunder that seemed to shake the earth. Surprised and terrified, the enemy fled in panic and confusion. The men of Israel pursued and slew them as they retreated to their own land. The battle was over! Once again Jehovah had been merciful and had spared His people from their dreaded foe.

That day I took a stone and set it up near Mizpah. I named it Ebenezer (EB-en-E-zer) or the "stone of help." It was a reminder to our nation that "thus far has the Lord helped us." After that there was peace in Israel for many years, and the Philistines did not invade our land again. When I returned to my home in Ramah (RA-mah), I built an altar there in gratitude to our God for all the mercy He had shown His people.

What joy and blessing I have known as a prophet of the

Lord. To feel His presence and to listen for His voice speaking to me—these have been the most awesome and wonderful experiences of my life. And all He asks of me is that I obey His commands and trust His wisdom. How great is our Jehovah God!

✳ ✳ ✳ ✳

Scripture References:
1 Samuel 2:18–35; 3:1–18; 7:5–17 (written in the tenth century B.C.); Hebrews 11:32

Spiritual Reflections:
Samuel was the last and greatest of the judges and the first of the prophets. He was considered by many in Old Testament times as the most important figure since the time of Moses. He anointed the first two kings of ancient Israel, Saul and David.

> Speak, O blessed Master, in this quiet hour,
>   Let me see Thy face, Lord, feel Your touch of pow'r.
> Fill me with the knowledge of Your glorious will;
>   All Thine own good pleasure in my life fulfill.
> —E. May Grimes

"Blessed indeed are those ears which listen not for the voice sounding without, but for the truth teaching inwardly. Blessed are the eyes that are shut to outward things but intent on things inward. Blessed are they who are glad to have time to spare for God, and who shake off all worldly hindrances. Consider these things, O my soul, and hear what the Lord your God speaks."
—Thomas a' Kempis (1379–1471)

Suggested Hymns:
- "Lord, Speak to Me"
- "O Jesus, I Have Promised"

Drama 18

Elijah

Come and see what God has done, how awesome His works in man's behalf! (Psalm 66:5).

When Ahab (A-hab) became ruler of the Northern Kingdom of Israel, he did more evil than any king before him. He provoked Jehovah by setting up an altar for the pagan god Baal and encouraging the people to worship there. One day a message from the Lord came to me. I was to go to the palace and tell the king, "As the Lord, the God of Israel, lives, whom I serve, there will be neither dew nor rain in the next few years except by my word."

After I delivered this message, the king and the idolatrous Queen Jezebel (JEZ-e-bel) were so angry that I was forced to escape to save my life. I hastened to the secluded region east of the Jordan and hid myself by a little brook. Here God miraculously cared for me as the ravens provided daily food and the brook supplied clear water. But then the drought that I had foretold to the king reached that area. It dried up my brook and forced me to move on. I traveled north to the town of Zarephath (ZAR-e-fath), where God assured me that I would find there a Canaanite woman who would provide for my needs. When I saw a poor woman at the city gates trying to gather a few sticks for a fire, I timidly asked her for some bread and water. She was reluctant to grant my request. Because of the severe drought she had only enough food remaining for one last meal for herself and her son before they would both face starvation. I assured her that if she would only trust the God of Israel, her supply of food and oil would not fail for the duration of the famine.

I went to stay at the widow's home and for a time all went well. As promised, her jar of flour was not used up nor did the jug of oil run dry. One day, however, God allowed another calamity to occur. Without warning, the widow's son became ill and died, and for some reason the mother felt that I was to blame for this death. "What do you have against me?" she questioned indignantly. "Did you come to remind me of my sin and kill my only child?"

"Give me your son," I replied. I carried him to the upper room and laid him on his bed. Then I prayed earnestly, "O Lord my God, let this boy's life return to him!" And the Lord heard my cry for the child's life was miraculously restored. The mother was overjoyed when I presented the boy to her. "Now I know that you are a man of God," she exclaimed, "and that the word of the Lord from your mouth is the truth."

After three years, the Lord told me to return to King Ahab to tell him that there would once again be rain in the land. The king was shocked to see me since he had been searching frantically to have me put to death. He shouted angrily, "Is it you, Elijah, you troubler of Israel?" I told the king that he was the troubler—not I—because he had abandoned the Lord's commands and followed after Baal.

I proposed a challenge to Ahab. At Mount Carmel, Jehovah, the God of Israel, would oppose the 450 prophets of Baal as well as the 400 additional prophets who feasted daily at Jezebel's table. I told the people that the time had come for them to choose whom they were going to worship. "How long will you waver between two opinions?" I asked. "If the Lord is God, follow Him; but if Baal is God, then follow him." The people were strangely silent.

We began our contest with the 850 prophets against me, Jehovah's lone remaining prophet. I instructed those false prophets to begin calling their god, and when they had finished, I would call upon the name of the Lord. And the one who answered by fire . . . LET HIM BE GOD!

From morning to evening the frantic prophets cried out to Baal. "O Baal," they shouted, "answer us!" They danced upon their altar and even slashed themselves with knives till the blood flowed freely. Still no response came from Baal. I couldn't resist taunting them, "Shout louder . . . perhaps Baal is deep in thought . . . or busy . . . or traveling . . . or maybe he is sleeping and must be awakened."

When they were finished, I called the people together. I

began by repairing the Lord's altar, which had long been neglected. I also took twelve stones and placed them on the altar as a reminder to the people that they were still a part of God's kingdom. Then I ordered that everything be thoroughly drenched with water. I lifted my voice to the Almighty, "God of Abraham, Isaac and Jacob, let it be known this day that You are God in Israel and that I am Your servant and have done these things at Your command. Answer me, O Lord, so these people will know that You are turning their hearts back once again."

Even as I spoke, flames consumed the sacrifice, the wood, the stones, and even the water! The people fell on their faces and humbly acknowledged Jehovah as their God. I ordered that the false prophets be put to death in obedience to God's command that whoever sacrificed to any god other than the Lord must be destroyed.

When the king told Queen Jezebel that I had all of her favored prophets killed, she was furious. She commanded my execution immediately. Once again I had to flee quickly to save my life. I made my way to the desert, where I sank into feelings of deep despair and exhaustion under a small shade tree. I complained to God that I had been through enough and now wished to die. At that moment an angel of the Lord appeared and revived my spirit with special nourishment.

Later the angel returned and told me to travel to Mount Horeb (HOR-eb), the mountain where God had appeared to Moses. For forty days and nights I traveled on wearily until at last I found a resting place in the mountain. While I lay there in despair, the voice of God again spoke to me. I was told to stand on the mountainside where the Almighty's glory would be revealed. And what an awesome display of power it was! First there was a mighty wind that shook the very rocks, then an earthquake, and finally a blazing fire. But then I heard merely a small, soft whisper . . . and I knew this was the true voice of God. With Him at my side, I realized that I had no further cause for discouragement.

After that the Lord informed me that my service for Him would not be complete until I had anointed another prophet to be my successor. I traveled along the Jordan Valley until

God guided me to a man named Elisha busily plowing his fields. When I placed my cloak around him, he left his oxen and prepared to follow me as my constant companion.

How good Jehovah God has been throughout my years of service for Him. Even during my many times of despair and self-pity, He has always been patient and merciful. Throughout eternity I will praise His Holy Name.

✽ ✽ ✽ ✽

Scripture References:
>Exodus 22:20; 1 Kings 17:1–24; 18:1–45; 19:1–21; 2 Kings 1–2; Luke 4:25; James 5:17

Spiritual Reflections:
- Elijah was the first great prophet to the Northern Kingdom of Israel. His mission spans approximately fifteen years, from about 865 to 850 B.C.
- Elijah has been titled "the grandest and most romantic character Israel ever produced."
- Elijah and his successor Elisha are the Scripture's greatest miracle workers between Moses and Jesus.
- God rewarded Elijah by translating him by a whirlwind into heaven. Only one other person, Enoch, was taken by God without having to pass through the experience of death (Gen. 5:24; 2 Kings 2:11–12).
- According to Malachi 4:5, it is believed by many that Elijah will once again return to earth to restore the Jewish people to God "before that great and dreadful day of the Lord comes."

Suggested Hymns:
- "Does Jesus Care?"
- "Come, Ye Disconsolate"

Drama 19

The Shunammite (SHOO-nam-ite) Woman

He who refreshes others will himself be refreshed (Proverbs 11:25).

"Go quickly and ask the prophet Elisha if he would join us for our noontime meal," I instructed one of my servants. Often as I sat sewing by my window, I had observed God's noted prophet when he passed our way. He and his servant frequently traveled this hot and dusty road between Samaria and Mount Carmel as they pursued their many duties. How pleased we were when Elisha consented to dine with us. After the first time he and his servant continued to stop for refreshment whenever they visited our little village of Shunem (SHOO-nem).

Since my husband was a man of means and our home was a spacious one, I began thinking that we should do even more for this holy man of God. With my husband's consent I prepared for Elisha a comfortable little room on the roof of our home. Here he could rest whenever he desired.

One evening as he reclined in his cool room, Elisha sent his servant Gehazi (ge-HA-zi) to tell me, "Since you have gone to all this trouble for us, now my master asks what can be done for you? Would you like to have him speak on your behalf to the king or perhaps the commander of the army for a position of honor for your husband?"

"Oh, no," I answered in surprise. "We are satisfied with our home here among our own people and need nothing more for a better life."

In a little while Gehazi returned to say that Elisha wished to speak to me personally. I went up and stood in the doorway of his little rooftop room. The voice of the prophet rang out, "About this time next year you will hold a son in your arms."

I was startled. "Oh, no, my lord, do not mislead your servant . . . . Oh man of God!" I trembled with joy at the thought of such a blessing. For many years my greatest desire had been to have a child. But my husband was getting older, and such an event seemed impossible to us. The following year, to our amazement, our lovely son was born! He became the joy of our lives. We never ceased praising Almighty God for His priceless gift of love.

Sometimes the course of our lives is difficult to understand. As our boy grew older, his father enjoyed having his son's company in the fields watching the reapers at work. One morning as they walked along in the hot sun, our boy suddenly cried out with a blinding pain in his head. A few moments later he collapsed. Immediately he was carried home to me, and I cared for him as tenderly as I could. By noontime, however, as I held him I could see that he was slowly sinking, until soon he stopped breathing and slipped away.

Stunned and scarcely believing that he was really dead, I cried out to Jehovah God for help! Instantly I felt calm again and I knew what I should do. I carried my lifeless son to the prophet Elisha's room and laid him on the bed. Hurrying to my husband, I requested a servant and a donkey so that I might go to the man of God as quickly as possible. "Lead on and do not slow down unless I tell you," I instructed my servant as we sped to Mount Carmel where the prophet was staying. As we approached, his servant Gehazi ran to greet us. "Are you all right?" he asked excitedly, "Is your husband all right? Is your child all right?"

"Everything is well," I answered abruptly, pushing on ahead to Elisha himself. I fell at the prophet's feet while all the time Gehazi tried to restrain me.

"Leave her alone," commanded the prophet. "She is in bitter distress, but the Lord has not told me why."

"Did I ask you for a son, my lord?" I cried out. "Didn't I tell you, 'Do not raise my hopes?'" As I shared my grief, Elisha directed his servant to run with all speed to lay the prophet's staff on the boy's face. But I appealed to the prophet,

"As surely as the Lord lives and as you live, I will not leave you." After I urged him further, Elisha returned to my home with me. On the way Gehazi met us and reported sadly, "I laid your staff on the boy's face but he has not awakened."

When we arrived at our home, Elisha hurried to his room and closed the door. I waited below patiently, lifting my eyes to God in earnest prayer. In spite of my heavy sorrow, the assurance of God's goodness gave me peace—but how the moments dragged on. Then Gehazi appeared saying, "Come."

Up to the prophet's room I ran . . . and saw my precious child standing there alive. When Elisha said, "Take your son," I bowed myself at the prophet's feet. Then I called the rest of the household to join us in a time of grateful praise to God.

How unsearchable are the ways of Jehovah and the unfailing love He shows to those who place their trust in Him!

❊ ❊ ❊ ❊

Scripture Reference:

2 Kings 4:8–37 (written in the sixth century B.C., records the fall of the Northern Kingdom of Israel in 721 B.C. and the fall of Judah with the destruction of Jerusalem in 586 B.C. as well as the mighty ministry of Elisha)

Spiritual Reflections:

After Elijah's translation to heaven, Elisha became the dominant religious figure in Israel during the remainder of his life.

It should be noted that this mother's lifetime friendship with the prophet began with a simple act of hospitality. Consider anew the Christian's responsibility for exercising this gift (Rom. 12:13; 1 Timothy 3:2; Titus 1:8; 1 Peter 4:9.

Suggested Hymns:
- "Like a River Glorious"
- "For the Beauty of the Earth"

Mephibosheth (Me-FIB-o-sheth)

He who conceals his sins does not prosper, but whoever confesses and renounces them finds mercy (Proverbs 28:13).

"Take the child and run! Saul and Jonathan are dead!" This cry was one of my earliest memories, as my nurse picked me up in her arms and fled from the palace. But in her frenzy the poor woman somehow stumbled and dropped me on the marble steps. So at the age of five I was crippled for life in both feet. My grandfather King Saul and my father Jonathan had both gone out to battle against the Philistines and were defeated. I was taken away and hidden in the obscure little village of Lodebar (lo-DEE-bar), far from the royal palace.

There for many years I lived a quiet life. In time I married and had a child. No one, however, ever seemed aware of my royal parentage. But one day, to my surprise, there came a messenger from King David summoning me to his imperial palace. I was terrified for it was customary for a new king to destroy all the men of the royal family that had reigned before him. As I approached the great throne of our king, I bowed low, pleading, "I am your servant."

"Do not be afraid," said King David as he reached his hand toward me. "For I will surely show kindness for the sake of your father Jonathan. I will restore to you all the land that belonged to your grandfather Saul . . . and you will always eat at my table."

"What is your servant," I stammered, "that you should notice a dead dog like me?" But it all came true. From then on my family and I lived in the palace as King David's very own family. All of my restored lands were farmed and harvested by a former servant of grandfather Saul, a man named Ziba (ZI-bah). My growing devotion and gratitude to our king was inexpressible!

But life is filled with unexpected changes. How grieved we all were during that fearful time when David's third son Absalom (AB-sa-lom) conspired against his father with the intent of seizing the throne. King David felt it necessary to flee from his palace, taking with him the entire household except for a few women caretakers. However, without telling David, I chose to stay behind. I'm really not certain why. I surely loved the king with all my soul, but I wanted to wait in the palace to see how the battle with Absalom would go. I was actually a coward. In spite of all David had done for me, I failed him at a time when he needed my support. My motives were purely selfish!

One day word came that my steward Ziba was being disloyal to me. He had showered the king with generous gifts and reported to him that I had secretly stayed behind. He told David that I was hoping Absalom would win the battle and would then exalt me by restoring my grandfather Saul's kingdom to Israel. Angrily David declared me guilty of treason. He gave permission to Ziba to take all of my property and possessions. Soon came the news of fierce battles being fought, the sudden death of Absalom, and then the agonizing mourning of David for his beloved son.

I was deeply distressed . . . and truly remorseful. The king must surely believe that I was disloyal and no longer had any love for him. I was ashamed of my lack of courage and faithfulness. Without taking time to shave, dress my crippled feet, or wash my clothes, I rode off rapidly on a donkey to the River Jordan to await King David on his journey home. When the king saw me, he asked sternly, "Mephibosheth, why didn't you go with me?"

Haltingly I tried to explain my actions to him. I confessed I was ashamed that I had been disloyal after all his kindness to me when I was so undeserving. Realizing I had no reason to expect his forgiveness, I pleaded, "What right have I to make any more appeals to the king?"

There was a hushed pause as the king observed my grief-stricken face and disheveled appearance. David did not try to reprimand me further or humiliate me. Rather he seemed to brush off my feeble explanations with a gesture that said, "Why say more." I knew that in spite of all that had been reported about me, I was forgiven. The king turned to Ziba and ordered him to give back to me one half of my fields and possessions.

How gracious and compassionate David was. I realized that my great king understood and forgave my weakness and ingratitude. Earnestly I cried, "Let Ziba take everything now that my lord the king has arrived home safely." I freely gave up all my wealth. I was content merely to have the favor of my beloved David once more. I vowed in my heart that I would forever from that time on be faithful and devoted to my king!

✳ ✳ ✳ ✳

Scripture References:
    2 Samuel 4:4; 9:1–12; 16:1–4; 19:24–30

Spiritual Reflections:
    People with disabilities often fulfill a unique place in God's kingdom. Do we in the Christian community do all that we can to show compassion to those in our area who are differently abled? Give suggestions for improving this ministry.

Suggested Hymns:
    • "Blest Be the Tie That Binds"
    • "There's a Wideness in God's Mercy"

Drama 21

Naaman

How awesome are Your deeds! . . . all the earth bows
down to You (Psalm 66:3).

How unexpectedly the circumstances of our lives can change.
I felt that I had everything I could possibly desire—riches, a
loving family, prestige as a victorious general in the mighty
Syrian army, and a position of stature as a close friend of
our King Aram (A-ram). Life was truly wonderful, I thought.

Then one morning as I prepared to bathe, I noticed a
small white spot on my skin. At first I tried to ignore it, but
each day the sore grew worse. Finally I faced the truth . . . I
was a leper! I was forced to admit that I had the most
loathsome, deadly disease known to man. In despair I made
plans to leave my devoted family, my luxurious
surroundings, and my exalted position. I was destined to
spend my remaining years in isolation with only pain and
ugliness as my companions. I was devastated! Even my
faithful king could offer no help.

At that time my wife had a loyal and compassionate young
Jewish maid, who had been captured from Israel. The girl
told us she remembered that near her home in Samaria was
a prophet who was able to heal people of incurable diseases.
Could this really be true? Was it just a false rumor or a
result of the little maid's imagination? But I felt desperate
for help of any kind. When I consulted with King Aram, he
urged me, "By all means go, Naaman. I will send for you a
letter of introduction to the King of Israel." With this letter
as well as 750 pounds of silver, 150 pounds of gold, and a
number of my servants, I began the long and tedious journey
to Samaria.

When we finally arrived at Israel's royal palace, I presented
Aram's letter. At first the Jewish monarch was greatly
disturbed by it and tore his robes, for he thought it was an

attempt by King Aram to begin a quarrel and a possible war. Word was then sent to Elisha, the prophet we had heard about, who responded briefly, "Have the man come to me and he will know that there is a prophet in Israel."

As we arrived at Elisha's home some time later, I became irritated and impatient and wished I had never left Damascus. Instead of coming out to welcome me, Elisha merely sent his servant with this curt message: "Go wash yourself seven times in the Jordan River. Your flesh will be restored and you will be cleansed."

How angry and insulted I felt! Wash in that narrow muddy river? Our own rivers in Damascus were far superior. Couldn't I have bathed in one of those without the long tedious trek to this strange land? I turned in disgust to return home, feeling weary and ill. But my faithful servants ran after me and pleaded earnestly. Even though I was disappointed that the prophet had not asked me to perform some greater ritual, they appealed to me to at least try the distasteful instructions before leaving. At first my pride made me refuse. Then I recalled how trusting in Elisha's powers our young maid had been. And I had become desperate! Finally I decided to humble myself and do as the prophet had ordered.

I was exhausted by the time we arrived at the Jordan. I felt foolish and doubtful as I stepped slowly and cautiously into the dark and dirty river. Supporting me on each side, my servants helped me count . . . one, two, three, four, dipping nervously each time . . . five, six. I paused and took a deep breath before sinking hastily into the water for the seventh time. Did I dare open my eyes? As I rose from the water, surprised gasps from my attendants greeted me. Cautiously I peered at my skin. Could it be true? Everywhere my skin was as clear and perfect as that of a young man. "Oh joy, oh what wonder, I am healed!" I shouted jubilantly. "Thanks be to the God Jehovah of Israel!"

We made our way speedily to the house of Elisha, and this time the prophet was waiting to greet us. "Now I know that there is no God in all the world except in Israel," I cried out to him. "Please accept these gifts from your servant." But even though I urged him repeatedly, Elisha refused to take any reward for my healing. As we made preparation to return to Syria, the gracious prophet simply said, "Go in peace." Then I asked him if I could take with me as much earth as a pair of mules could carry. I desired that I might always be able to worship the Lord God on Israelite soil. And praise be to Jehovah, my life from that day has been filled with His peace.

✳ ✳ ✳ ✳

Scripture References:
    2 Kings 5:1–27; Luke 4:27

Spiritual Reflections:
    "The first test of a truly great person is his or her humility."   —John Ruskin

    "They that know God will be humble and they that know themselves cannot be proud."   —John Flavel

Suggested Hymns:
    • "Whiter Than Snow"
    • "Jesus Paid It All"

Esther

For how can I bear to see disaster fall on my people?
(Esther 8:6).

How sorrowful our people were! We were Jews living in foreign captivity, having been driven from our homeland in Palestine by the Babylonian King, Nebuchadnezzar (NEB-u-kad-NEZ-er). After his defeat we were placed under the rule of the mighty Persian empire, a kingdom that reached from Ethiopia to India and included people of nearly every race and language. Soon after my arrival here in Persia, both of my parents died. However, my older Jewish cousin, Mordecai (MOR-de-ki), adopted me as his daughter. I grew up in affluent surroundings since my cousin's recognized skills and abilities had gained for him a position of importance in the Persian palace.

The king of this vast Persian empire was the mighty Xerxes (ZURK-ses), who ruled his people with absolute and ruthless power. One day Mordecai told me that King Xerxes now wanted a new wife to reign as queen instead of the lovely Vashti (VASH-ti), who had recently fallen from his favor. A contest was to be held throughout all the provinces of the kingdom to find the fairest beauty in the empire. How shocked I was when my cousin announced that he was entering me in this competition. I had no desire to do this, yet out of respect for my foster father, I agreed.

After viewing all the many beautiful women brought before him, the king chose me as his queen and placed the royal crown on my head. I was astonished but, of course, gratified! King Xerxes celebrated further by having for all of his princes a great feast, which he called "Esther's Feast." In my honor the king gave expensive gifts to all of the provinces.

Everything went well for the next five years. I enjoyed the luxury of the court and the respect of the people. Although I could no longer visit him personally, I always kept in touch with my cousin through my chamberlain and the maids who attended me. During this time one of the ministers of the court named Haman (HA-man) had become especially popular with the king and had been appointed as the prime minister of the empire. The king further decreed that from now on everyone must pay Haman honor by bowing before him whenever he appeared in public.

One day I was greatly saddened when my attendants reported that they had seen Mordecai sitting at the city gates in great distress. They told me that my cousin had steadfastly refused to bow before the devious Haman. In revenge, this wicked perpetrator had now tricked the king into preparing an edict that would cause my cousin to be hanged and every Jewish person throughout the empire killed! That I was a Jewess was still unknown at the court.

I was horrified and fearful! But what could I do? I knew that if I went before the king uninvited, the penalty for such an action could be my death. Still reports kept coming that my cousin was depending on me to save our Jewish people from annihilation. One day I received this startling message from him: "If you remain silent at this time, relief and deliverance for the Jews will arise from another place, but you and your family will perish. And who knows but that you have come to royal position for such a time as this?"

I knew that I could remain silent no longer. I sent this word to Mordecai: "Go, gather together all the Jews who are in this city, and fast for me. Do not eat or drink for three days or nights. My maids and I will fast as you do. When this is done, I will go to the king, even though it is against the law. And if I perish, I perish!"

At the end of three days, I made my way timidly to the pillared hall . . . approached and faced the king. He was astonished to see me! But he held out the golden scepter, indicating that he would listen to my requests. I asked him meekly if he and his prime minister Haman would come to a special banquet I was having prepared for them that evening. He readily accepted. At the end of the banquet the king asked me, "What is your petition? It shall be granted."

I answered that I would like to have another such banquet for both of them the next night. Again he readily agreed.

After that first banquet, because King Xerxes was unable to sleep, he asked to have a history of his reign read to him by one of his attendants. He heard for the first time the account of how Mordecai had earlier saved the king's life from two officers who had plotted to kill him. Xerxes was so grateful to hear this that he immediately issued a decree that Mordecai should receive the full honors long overdue him.

While we were enjoying our second banquet, the king again asked me, "Queen Esther, what is your petition? What is your request? It will be given you; even to half the kingdom it will be granted!"

"O King, and if it pleases your majesty," I pleaded, "grant me my life—this is my petition. And spare my people—this is my request. For I and my people have been sold for destruction, slaughter and annihilation. If we had merely been sold as male and female slaves, I would have kept quiet, because no such distress would justify disturbing the king." Angrily, the king shouted, "Who is he? Where is the man who has dared to do such a thing?"

"The adversary and enemy is this vile Haman," I answered.

The furious king made a decree that Haman should be hanged immediately on the very gallows that he had just readied for Mordecai. King Xerxes further decreed that the Jewish people in every city and province throughout the empire now had the right to assemble whenever they desired. Also they were to be protected from any enemy who tried to harm them.

After that my cousin became greatly honored and was placed in a position of second in command to the king. He was also highly esteemed by the Jewish people throughout the empire for all that he had done in caring for them. Each year since then our Jewish people have held a special day to celebrate with feasting and joy the deliverance and freedom that is now ours.

Once again Jehovah God has been merciful to His chosen people. Blessed be His Holy Name!

❋ ❋ ❋ ❋

Scripture Reference:
   The book of Esther, written in the fifth century B.C.

Spiritual Reflections:
   Though the name of God is not mentioned in this book, in no other portion of the Bible is God's providential care of His chosen people more evident. The Jews still commemorate this deliverance in their yearly festival, Purim.
   How can this concept of each individual's uniqueness and importance in God's kingdom (Esther 4:14) be impressed upon believers today?

Suggested Hymns:
   • "Immortal, Invisible, God Only Wise"
   • "Great Is Thy Faithfulness"

David

I will sing and make music with all my soul . . . I
will praise You, O Lord, among the nations (Psalm
108:1, 3).

I have become known among our people as "the sweet singer
of Israel" because of my great love for music and my ability
to compose hymns of praise and worship to Almighty God.
Often I played and sang these songs as a boy when I was
alone under the stars among the sheep. Because of this, they
also call me "the shepherd king." I don't mind. I still
remember well the years I spent in my father's pastures
tending the flocks. It was there that I learned to know God
intimately and to trust Him with my very life. My struggles
and triumphs over the lion and bear in the fields near
Bethlehem and, of course, that miraculous victory over
fearsome Goliath further confirmed my confidence in my
Heavenly Father's love and care for me.

Then during the years that I spent in the palace with
King Saul, when often the only thing that could soothe his
troubled spirit was the playing of my harp, again it was
God's watchful protection that preserved and prepared me
for a position that He had destined for me—the throne of
Israel.

But my troubles were not over after I was crowned king.
Sorrow and conflict seemed to plague me constantly. There
was the loss of my devoted and loyal friend, Jonathan, whom
I loved as a brother, a war with the house of Saul, constant
battles with neighboring enemies, the heart-rending loss of
my infant child, and then my son Absalom! But I knew that
God had anointed me to the throne of Israel and had exalted
our kingdom to be a model of His goodness to all the heathen
nations of the world. And though we His people have often
failed Him, Jehovah, our covenant keeping God, has never

once forsaken us. Step by step He guides, much like a loving shepherd tenderly leading His sheep.

It still amazes me that my humble songs of devotion to God have now become the hymns of praise and adoration used by our people in their tabernacle worship. Among our pagan neighbors, our people have become widely known for their singing faith. Our services of worship each Sabbath Day are alive with psalms of praise that we both sing and play to the glory of our God.

I have always tried to encourage our people with this truth: God's people in every generation should be known as people of joy and thanksgiving. We should praise Jehovah often for His acts of power; praise Him for His surpassing greatness; praise Him with the sounding of the trumpets; praise Him with the strings and flutes; praise Him with the clash of the cymbals; and praise Him even with the resounding cymbals. Yes, let everything that has breath . . . PRAISE THE LORD!

* * * *

Scripture References:
    Psalm 150; Hebrews 11:32

Spiritual Reflections:
    David was Israel's mighty warrior, empire builder, king, and master musician of praise. Throughout the Bible his name appears more than one thousand times, more than that of any other character.

A psalm is a poem meant to be sung to the accompaniment of musical instruments. Psalms was no doubt used as a Jewish hymnal and is the longest book in the Bible. Nearly one half of these 150 psalms are believed to have been written by David from about the tenth century B.C. and later. The predominant theme of the entire book is that of praise.

The Bible speaks even more often about the value of praise in a believer's life than it does about the importance of prayer.

"There is no better remedy for murmuring and discontent than lifting the voice in true praise to God."
—author unknown

There is an old Jewish legend about the origin of praise. After God created mankind, says the legend, He asked the angels what they thought of the world He had made. "Only one thing is lacking," they said. "It is the sound of praise to the Creator." So, the story continues, God created music, the voices of birds, the whispering wind, the murmuring ocean, and planted melody in the people's hearts.

—anonymous

"Never let us forget that praise is to be the keynote, the beginning, the middle and end of every prayer."
—James S. Stewart

Suggested Hymns:
- "Praise to the Lord, the Almighty"
- "The Lord's My Shepherd, I'll Not Want"

Drama 24
Daniel

But Daniel resolved not to defile himself (Daniel 1:8).

Exiled in a heathen land—this was my fate for most of my adult life. As a young man I saw our beautiful city of Jerusalem besieged by the powerful Babylonian empire under the rule of Nebuchadnezzar (NEB-u-kad-NEZ-er). Our holy temple was looted, and ten thousand of our most talented and skilled Jewish people were taken captive. I was one of them. Only the poor of the land remained.

Soon after we were taken to Babylon, three of my companions and I were chosen to serve in the imperial court. Our Jewish names were changed so that I became Belteshazzar (BEL-te-shaz-er) rather than Daniel, while my friends were now known as Shadrach (SHA-drak), Meshach (ME-shak), and Abednego (a-BED-ne-go). We began an intensive three year training that included learning to speak and write Aramaic and mastering all of the scientific and diplomatic skills needed for court life. The king also decreed that we must develop our bodily strength as well as our minds. He ordered that we be nourished on the richest food and finest wines available. However, I didn't feel right about partaking of this heathen diet. I insisted that we would nourish our bodies only on vegetables and water. We were given a ten day trial. To the surprise of the king, after the trial period we were better in appearance and health than anyone else. We were allowed to continue our limited diet.

I began to realize that God had given me the gift of wisdom to interpret the dreams and visions of others. One day Nebuchadnezzar summoned all of his wisest men to help him understand a recent dream that was disturbing him. When these men were unable to help, the king became furious and threatened to execute all of the wise men in

Babylon. When I heard of this, I approached the king and begged him to give me time to reveal the interpretation. I gathered my three companions together and asked them to pray. And our prayer was answered. That night God revealed to me an interpretation of the king's mysterious dream. I told Nebuchadnezzar that his kingdom would not last forever, but eventually the God of heaven would set up a kingdom which would never be destroyed. Astonished with my ability, the king declared that the God of the Jews was God of all gods. He made me the head of the Babylonian wise men as well as ruler over the province of Babylon itself.

But King Nebuchadnezzar soon forgot his devotion to Jehovah God. He made a large idol of gold and demanded that everyone worship it. Death by burning was the punishment given to those who did not comply. When my three companions steadfastly refused to worship the idol, the king was furious! He ordered that these defiant leaders were to be placed in a furnace seven times hotter than normal. But when the three Jewish men were released, not a hair of their heads was singed, nor their robes scorched, nor was there the slightest smell of smoke on them! How surprised everyone was! Once again the king acknowledged Jehovah God by declaring, "Praise be to the God of Shadrach, Meshach and Abednego, who has sent His angel and delivered His servants who trusted in Him." The king promoted my three companions to even greater positions of importance in the government.

After a long reign, Nebuchadnezzar was replaced on the throne by his son, Belshazzar (bel-SHAZZ-ar). One evening this young king was holding a great feast and drinking wine from the sacred vessels that had been plundered from the temple in Jerusalem. Suddenly, while everyone was making merry, a man's hand appeared and wrote with its finger on the palace wall. Terrified, the king tried desperately to find someone to interpret the mysterious words. When none of the court's wise men could decipher the writing, the king sent for me. I knew immediately what the words meant. God was telling the young ruler that his reign was about to end because he had abused the temple vessels and had set himself up against the Lord of heaven. That same night Belshazzar was murdered when Darius (da-RI-us), the King of the Medes, invaded Babylon and captured the kingdom.

Although by this time I was an old man, King Darius appointed me as one of his three presidents to rule over the empire for him. It wasn't long, however, before some of my rivals became envious of my new position. They approached the king with an edict to sign. It decreed that for a thirty day period no one could pray to any god or man but Darius himself. Offenders would be placed into a den of lions, and once the document was signed, not even the king himself could change it.

I refused to acknowledge this decree. My entire life had been a life of prayer to God, and I would not change even with the threat of lions. When his followers caught me praying, the king had no choice. He ordered that I be thrown into the lions' den. Early the next morning when the troubled king appeared, he was amazed to find me alive and well. I told him that my God had sent His angel to shut the lions' mouths. The king ordered that my rivals who had plotted against me be thrown into the den, where they were immediately crushed! King Darius issued this decree at once and sent it to every part of his kingdom: "People must fear and reverence the God of Daniel."

During these later years of my life, I have continued to experience dreams and visions regarding the future course of world history and the final judgment. I foresee occurring a time of great distress such as never known before. This will be followed by the everlasting glory of the saints. Those whose names are written in the Book will be delivered, and they will continue to shine like the brightness of the heavens.

Praise be to the name of God forever and ever. He gives wisdom to the wise and knowledge to the discerning.

* * * *

Scripture References:
    The book of Daniel, written in the sixth century B.C.; Matthew 24:15; Luke 1:19, 26; Hebrews 11:33–34

Spiritual Reflections:
Faithfulness to God can bring success even under the most adverse circumstances.

"To myself will I show a heart of steel,
To my fellow man a heart of love,
To my God a heart of flame."

—Augustine

"Do not go where the path may lead; go instead where there is no path and leave a trail."

—author unknown

Suggested Hymns:
- "Dare to Be a Daniel"
- "Who is on the Lord's Side?"

Drama 25

Amos

The sovereign Lord has spoken—who can but prophesy?
(Amos 3:8).

How can people be deeply religious, practice all of the correct rituals and ceremonies, and still treat their fellow men with disrespect and cruelty? This is a matter that has often been disturbing to me.

One day here in our little region near Bethlehem, while tending my herd of sheep and caring for my grove of fig trees, I was overcome once again with these thoughts. Now I have never claimed to be a recognized prophet nor have I been trained for this ministry in a prophet's school. But that day I distinctly heard God's voice telling me that I should leave my home in Judah and travel to Samaria, the capital of our Northern Kingdom. There I was to prophesy to those people, warning them of a coming destruction and urging them to return to a true worship of the God of their fathers.

For the past twenty-five years the citizens of this Northern Kingdom had enjoyed a time of great prosperity and military expansion under the rule of Jeroboam (JER-o-BO-am) the Second. Though they still pretended to worship Jehovah, the people had become increasingly brazen in their idolatry and moral rottenness. Also the leaders neglected the peasants, who lived in utter poverty, while the rich became more greedy and merciless. I was shocked and angered when I saw these conditions.

I began traveling throughout the land with the message that rather than more pious practices, God desires a change of heart and manner of living. Repeatedly I told the people that a religion of ceremonies and rituals that is divorced from morality is something God abhors. On behalf of Jehovah I spoke these harsh words of warning: "I hate, I despise

96

your religious feasts; I cannot stand your assemblies. Even though you bring Me burnt offerings and grain offerings, I will not accept them. Though you bring choice fellowship offerings, I will have no regard for them. Away with the noise of your songs! I will not listen to the music of your harps. But let justice roll on like a river, righteousness like a never-failing stream."

On other occasions I pronounced God's further condemnation upon their way of living: "Woe to you who are complacent in Zion, and to you who feel secure in Mount Samaria, you notable men of the foremost nation . . . You lie on beds inlaid with ivory and lounge on your couches. You dine on choice lambs and fattened calves. You strum away on your harps like David and improvise on musical instruments. You drink wine by the bowlful and use the finest lotions, but you do not grieve over the needs of the afflicted. Therefore you will be among the first to go into exile; your feasting and lounging will end."

The people became very upset with me. I especially disturbed the religious leaders, who resided in Bethel (BETH-el), the religious center of the Northern Kingdom. One day the chief priest of Bethel's idolatrous temple sent this message to King Jeroboam: "Amos is raising a conspiracy against you in this very heart of Israel. The land cannot bear all his words." Then this apostate priest attacked me directly: "Get out you seer! Go back to the land of Judah. Earn your bread and do your prophesying there."

Before returning to Judah, I gave one final warning of the impending doom that awaited these people when they would be taken captive into a pagan exile. My words had no effect. I further prophesied that there was a brighter future ahead, however, when God would one day return His people Israel from their scattered captivity and restore them to their promised land, never again to be uprooted.

Upon my return home, I began to write all that God had told me. And though the prophetic events have not yet occurred, I know with certainty that the words of God are true. Blessed be the Lord, whose name is God Almighty!

✳✳✳✳

Scripture References:
   Amos 5:21–27; 6:1–7; 7:10–13; 9:11–15, written in the eighth century B.C.

Spiritual Reflections:
   It had been two hundred years since the Ten Tribes had separated from Judah and formed the Northern Kingdom. During this time much pagan idolatry had developed in their religious practices. Amos was one of the final voices sent by God to warn these people of their impending disaster. Within approximately thirty years after these pronouncements, the prosperous Northern Kingdom of Israel was crushed and taken into captivity by the cruel Assyrian army.
   Amos teaches forcibly the truth that the worship of God should produce real changes in the lives of believers, from the way they treat their fellow men to the most basic moral and ethical practices in everyday living.

Suggested Hymns:
   • "O Master, Let Me Walk with Thee"
   • "Rescue the Perishing"

Jonah

God . . . commands all people everywhere to repent (Acts 17:30).

As a young man in our small Galilean (GAL-i-LE-an) village near Nazareth, I sensed a call from God to be His prophet. I began ministering to my Jewish brethren of Israel's ten Northern Tribes, now ruled by King Jeroboam (JER-o-BO-am) the Second. The king considered me not only his spiritual leader but also one of his trusted statesmen. I have been instrumental in advising him as to how we can expand our kingdom by pushing back the boundaries of our enemies.

One of our most dreaded enemies is that powerful and ruthless Empire of Assyria with its ancient city, Nineveh (NIN-e-vah). This important capital city, widely known for its sinful practices, is so vast that it takes three days just to walk around it. It is truly one of the most impressive cities in the world.

Can you not understand my utter dismay when recently the voice of God told me that I should travel to Nineveh? I was to warn these people that the Almighty was about to destroy them in forty days if they did not repent of their wickedness and seek His forgiveness. I pleaded with God to relieve me of this mission, but to no avail. Finally it seemed that the only way I could escape His presence was to take a boat ride as far away from Nineveh as possible. I made my way to the Port of Joppa and found a ship about to sail for Tarshish (TAR-shish), located on the western end of the Mediterranean Sea.

It was so peaceful there on the water that soon I was fast asleep in the ship's quarters below. The next thing I remember was the captain of the ship awaking me rudely. He shouted that a violent storm had arisen, and he feared for the safety of his boat. I was ordered to get up quickly and start praying to my God! When I reached the deck, the sailors had decided to cast lots in order to find out who was responsible for this calamity. And their lot fell on me. They began questioning me frantically: "What is your occupation? Where do you come from? What is your country?" I told them that I was a Hebrew who worshiped Jehovah, the God of heaven, who made the sea and the land. They were terrified with my answer. "What have you done?" they screamed above the roar of the wild waves.

Deep within my soul I knew the reason for this storm. I told the sailors that the only way the storm would cease would be for them to throw me overboard. They protested and tried even harder to row the boat to land, but the waves only dashed higher! Soon I heard them cry out, "O Lord, do not let us die for taking this man's life; do not hold us accountable for killing an innocent man." And with that they threw me overboard. Immediately the raging sea grew calm.

Then occurred the most amazing miracle! As I struggled and gasped for breath in the depths of the sea, God sent a great fish that swallowed me and kept me safe in its stomach. When I realized what had happened, I began praying earnestly. I promised God that if He would spare my life, I would sacrifice to Him a song of thanksgiving, and what I had ever vowed to Him, I would make good. I knew as never before that my salvation came only from Jehovah God. After three long days and nights, the great fish spewed me out on dry land.

Once again I heard the voice of God telling me to go to Nineveh with the same message He had already given me. This time I did not hesitate. On my very first day in the city, I began walking through the streets proclaiming loudly, "Forty days and Nineveh will be overturned." No doubt the people had already heard of my miraculous deliverance from the sea, for without hesitation they believed God and repented of their sins. Even the king responded quickly by issuing this royal decree:

Let everyone call urgently on God. Let them give up their evil ways and their violence. Who knows? God may yet relent and with compassion turn from His fierce anger so that we will not perish.

And then the thing happened that I had secretly feared. God in His graciousness had compassion on those wicked people and did not bring upon them the destruction He had threatened. I felt absolutely discredited as a prophet. I couldn't understand why Jehovah would show mercy to a hostile heathen people who had always been intent on destroying us—His chosen people. I was so infuriated that I asked God to take my life. But the Lord simply responded, "Jonah, do you have any right to be angry?"

I made my way outside the gates, built a shelter to rest in, and waited to see what would happen to the city. Then God provided another miracle. A huge plant began growing next to my shelter, providing a cooling shade for my comfort. My joyous spirit was restored. But on the very next morning, God sent a worm which began chewing on this vine until it was completely withered. Even worse, the wind and sun that day were so unbearably hot that I became desperately ill. In my despair, I cried out to God that now it would surely be better for me to die than live. But once more God responded gently, "Jonah, do you really have a right to be angry about the vine?" In my fury I told Him that I did have this right and was truly angry enough to die.

Then God began teaching me an unforgettable lesson. He reminded me that the eternal souls of people are far more important than a prophet's pride and patriotism . . . or than the plants of the field that quickly grow and die. The heathen, even those non-Hebrew people of Nineveh, needed to hear and experience His love and forgiveness. I began to understand something of God's concern for that great city and people everywhere.

✳ ✳ ✳ ✳

Scripture References:
2 Kings 14:25; Matthew 12:38–42; 16:1–4; Luke 11:29–32; The book of Jonah, written in the eighth century B.C.

Spiritual Reflections:

The story of Jonah typifies the burial and resurrection of Christ as well as the giving of the Gospel to the Gentile world and the attitude of the Jews regarding this "whosoever gospel."

The insights one gains from this book about the character of God as well as the many practical applications for Christian living make this an invaluable study for every believer.

Suggested Hymns:
- "Trust and Obey"
- "In Christ There Is No East or West"

NEW TESTAMENT

Drama 27

Matthew

Be shepherds of God's flock . . . not greedy for money, but
eager to serve . . . being examples to the flock (1 Peter 5:2–3).

It was almost the end of another hectic business day. I was
counting the cash receipts and carefully recording the
necessary entries in my books when a stranger approached
my tax collecting booth, located on the busy Damascus Road
that runs between Bethsaida (beth-SA i-dah) and Capernaum
(ka-PUR-na-um). I looked up hurriedly and was about to
begin my usual tirade of haranguing with him, a practice I
have perfected through the years to extract the maximum
taxes from any individual. Suddenly I realized that this was
Jesus, the carpenter from Nazareth, the very man everyone
was discussing. They claimed that He was going about
helping and healing people, proclaiming that He had the
authority to forgive sins and provide the assurance of eternal
life.

Lately I had been thinking seriously about this matter of
forgiveness and the hereafter. Because of my business of
collecting taxes for the Roman government, most of my
Jewish acquaintances had come to view me as a scoundrel, a
traitor, and even a crook. However, I always thought of
myself as simply a shrewd business person doing a necessary
job that rewarded me well. As for my ancestry, I was raised
in the finest of Jewish homes and was taught in the traditions
of our faith and the writings of the prophets. So I always felt
that I was a God-fearing person, even though my fellow
Jews continued to shun me whenever I attended a synagogue.
They treated me as though I were nothing but a gentile
sinner.

But why would this Jesus be stopping to see me, I
wondered? Was He coming to give me more of those lectures
about honesty that I was always hearing from our religious

leaders? To my surprise He looked at me with such compassion and understanding that I suddenly felt very uneasy and unclean in His presence. And when Jesus began speaking, I felt drawn to Him and listened attentively to every word. Never had I known a man with such authority and yet with such tenderness.

Then Jesus spoke words that I will never forget. "Matthew, I would like to invite you to leave this tax collecting work to follow Me and be one of My disciples." For some time I was too shocked to respond . . . for this Man was actually seeking help from a despised publican like me! No longer did collecting taxes for Rome and accumulating personal wealth seem important. I closed my tax booth immediately, even leaving the money and records behind. As I walked away with Jesus, my life for the very first time seemed to have purpose and meaning.

In the days that followed I was so thrilled with my new life with the Master that it wasn't long before I wanted my other publican colleagues and influential leaders in this region to meet Jesus personally. I organized a great feast in my home and invited all of these people to attend. What an event that was! I was amazed that Jesus was as comfortable talking with this group about their need for repentance as He was with the lowliest person. It wasn't long, however, before the snide criticism from the many religious leaders in this area began spreading. "We don't understand," they said haughtily, "how this Jesus could claim to be sent from God and then sit at the same table with publicans and other evil people." Jesus' response was always clear and gracious. "It is not the healthy who need a doctor. I have not come to call the righteous but sinners to repentance."

During the next several years as I traveled about with the Lord and my fellow disciples, I realized more clearly each day that Jesus is truly the God-Man . . . the promised Messiah and the complete fulfillment of all that our prophets foretold! During this time I always tried to stay as close as I could to the Master. I wanted to hear and notate all that He said as well as to record accurately the events and miracles that occurred. I also spent much time tracing our Lord's ancestry back to King David and even to our ancient Father

Abraham—forty-two generations in all. How thrilled I was when I first grasped the truth that even as David was our great king of Jewish history, Jesus will be the King who will reign over His universal kingdom throughout eternity.

Since that day when Jesus invited me to leave my tax collecting, the desire of my life has been to share His transforming message with others—especially my Jewish kinsmen. The Lord's final challenge and promise to us disciples just before returning to His heavenly Father will always be my life's mission: "Go and make disciples of all nations, baptizing them in the name of the Father and of the Son and of the Holy Spirit, and teaching them to obey everything I have commanded you. And surely I am with you always, to the very end of the age."

✳ ✳ ✳ ✳

Scripture References:
   Matthew 9:9–13; 28:20 (written about A.D. 50); Luke 5:29–31

Spiritual Reflections:
   According to tradition, Matthew remained in Jerusalem for a number of years after the ascension before ministering in Persia and Macedonia. It is believed that he died a martyr's death in Ethiopia.

Suggested Hymns:
   • "Jesus Calls Us"
   • "O Zion, Haste"

Mark

Since my youth, O God, You have taught me (Psalm 71:17).

While still a young man, I was privileged to become known as a helper to the apostles of Jesus. I remember well that thrilling day when I first met Peter. I was with a large group of believers who were gathered in our Jerusalem home to pray for this revered leader. Herod, that cruel king, had just arrested some of the Christians in our local church with the intent of persecuting them. Already with the sword he had put to death James, the brother of John. And now, sensing that this vicious action was pleasing the Jewish masses, Herod proceeded to seize Peter as well and place him in prison under heavy guard.

While everyone was fervently praying for his release, there was a loud knock at the door. It was suddenly silent as we waited to see who it could be. My mother's servant girl, Rhoda, ran to answer. "Peter is at the door!" she shrieked.

"You're out of your mind," several shouted at her.

"You must be seeing Peter's angel," others sneered. But the knocking continued. Finally some of us opened the door cautiously, and there indeed was the apostle Peter himself! We threw our arms around him with loud cries of joy. Peter motioned for us to be quiet as he proceeded to tell us how the Lord loosed the chains around his wrists so that he could miraculously walk out of his prison cell without being noticed by the guards.

During the following months the apostle Peter and I became especially close friends, much like a father and son. He taught me the meaning of a personal relationship with Christ. As he related the many thrilling experiences and events he had shared with the Lord, I was fascinated with these accounts. The more he told me about the earthly ministry of our Lord, the more I admired Him. Jesus was a man of action whose supernatural deeds supported His teachings and demonstrated His deity to the people.

I also enjoyed an intimate relationship with the apostle Paul and his co-worker, Barnabas, who happened to be my cousin. These two men traveled throughout the Mediterranean-gentile world, preaching Christ and establishing local churches. I was much impressed with this action-filled ministry, and when they invited me to join them on their next trip, I readily accepted. I thoroughly enjoyed working with these spiritually gifted leaders. One day, however, I decided rather impulsively that I wanted to see my mother in Jerusalem. I left hurriedly and returned home without first telling my co-workers. The apostle Paul became very irritated with my immature action, and when plans were made for the next trip, Paul made it clear that he didn't want me along. The apostle excluded not only me, but also Barnabas, with whom he ended his long relationship. My cousin Barnabas and I continued together for a time and made a missionary trip to Cypress. Paul chose Silas as his new co-worker.

Some time later, however, when the beloved apostle Paul visited Jerusalem, he and I enjoyed a restored fellowship. He showed his confidence in me by using me as his emissary in ministering to churches when he was unable to be there in person. I felt very honored when the apostle wrote to Pastor Timothy that I was profitable to him for the ministry.

Several years later when I received word that Paul had been placed in a Roman prison for preaching the Gospel, I made my way there immediately in order to be of help to him. He was so pleased to have me at his side during this trying time that he wrote to the believers at Colosse (ko-LOS-ee) that I was one of the few among his fellow laborers who had been a comfort to him during the weary hours of his imprisonment.

While in Rome I learned that my spiritual father Peter was also imprisoned there for the sake of the Gospel. And now there is a strong rumor that both of these great pillars of the church are soon to be martyred. I am determined to spend every possible moment with them. I especially need to learn more from the apostle Peter about his time with the Lord. Our fellow believers here are most anxious to learn everything possible concerning the apostle's first-hand knowledge of Jesus' words and actions.

It is now my earnest intent to put these accounts into writing in order that everyone, especially the skeptical, unbelieving Gentiles, might know the accurate and glorious truths about Jesus, the Son of God, and by believing in Him may obtain eternal life.

✳ ✳ ✳ ✳

Scripture References:
> Acts 12:12; 13:13; 15:25; Colossians 4:10–11; 2 Timothy 4:11; 1 Peter 5:13; the gospel of Mark

Spiritual Reflections:
> The book of Mark was likely written in Rome near the time of the destruction of Jerusalem in A.D. 70. It has been called "the story of Jesus as remembered by Peter and recorded by Mark."

> After the deaths of Peter and Paul, tradition states that Mark visited Egypt, founded the church of Alexandria, and died as a martyr.

> Let none hear you idly saying,
>   'There is nothing I can do,'
> While the souls of men are dying,
>   and the Master calls for you.
> Take the task He gives you gladly;
>   let His work your pleasure be;
> Answer quickly when He calls you—
>   "Here Am I; Send Me, Send Me!"
>   —author unknown

Suggested Hymns:
- "Give of Your Best to the Master"
- "Work for the Night Is Coming"

Drama 29

Luke

Send forth Your light and Your truth, let them guide
me (Psalm 43:3).

My dream of becoming a medical doctor had been fulfilled,
and I enjoyed a busy practice in my native city of Antioch in
Syria. Yet somehow I began to feel restless. I realized that
there was a spiritual void in my life. As a gentile I had been
trained in my youth in the language and culture of the
Greeks. I began to read seriously some of the Greek writings
in the areas of philosophy and religion. One day I came
upon a copy of the Jewish Old Testament written in Greek.
As I poured over it, I became intrigued with the writings of
the Jewish prophets and desired to know more about this
unusual religion. About that time I heard that a man named
Paul had come to our city to lecture about his Jewish faith. I
was impressed when I heard that he had been a student of
the noted scholar, Rabbi Gamaliel (ga-Ma-li-el). I went eagerly
to hear this Paul speak.

But how surprised I was with his message. He related in
such a clear and forceful way his dramatic conversion
experience. And from that time on, Paul became a zealous
follower of Jesus Christ . . . preaching and teaching the Gospel
of grace to both Jew and Gentile and establishing new
congregations of believers everywhere.

I was much impressed with Paul's brilliance and his
devotion to Christ. I tried to spend as much time as I could
with this scholarly man in order to learn from him everything
possible about the Christian faith. Soon I was convinced that
Jesus is truly God's Son. I gladly owned Him as my Savior
and surrendered my life to His lordship.

The skills of my scientific education have, no doubt, given
me an inquiring mind, for once I became a believer, I
developed a passionate desire to learn first-hand every detail

about Jesus—from His birth to His ascension into heaven. I wasn't content merely to read or hear what others were saying about Him. My intent was to investigate and authenticate His life and ministry so completely that even those skeptical Grecian minds would be attracted to Him. I traveled the countryside extensively, looking for anyone who had ever had actual contact with Christ. I sought out His disciples and family members, especially His mother Mary. What thrilling accounts concerning the details of Jesus' birth were related by His mother . . . her espousal to Joseph, the angel's annunciation, the angelic chorus, the tender manger scene, and then her own song of praise to God. The more I learned and heard about my Lord, the more enthusiastic I became. I even spent considerable time tracing His earthly lineage back to Adam, our original father and God's first created son. My study and research have given me undeniable proof that every Old Testament prophecy about the birth and ministry of a promised Messiah was perfectly fulfilled in Christ. He is truly the Savior for all mankind!

My medical work has also helped me appreciate another quality of my Lord . . . His tender compassion for people. This was the very ideal I was taught in my training . . . to be genuinely concerned with every patient's welfare, regardless of the circumstances. This was perfectly demonstrated by the Lord. It made no difference to Him whether people were rich, poor, young, or old. . . . He simply ministered to their need. I like to think of Christ as truly the Great Physician of both soul and body.

I not only pursued my own historical study about Jesus, but also became involved in the ministry of the apostle Paul. I observed his zealous efforts to win converts to Christ and establish new congregations of believers. Our journeys took us to nearly every major Mediterranean city. How I loved and revered this gifted man of God! There was nothing I would not have done for him. Since Paul was not robust in health, God allowed me the privilege of caring for his bodily needs in order that he might give himself fully to the work of the Gospel. I was so pleased that when the apostle wrote to the Church at Colosse (ko-LOS-ee), he referred to me as his "beloved physician." And how God blessed his ministry during those final years of his life, despite persecutions, imprisonments and finally a martyr's death in Rome. The memory of this man's life has convinced me that the Gospel will only be established when people like him are willing to give their very lives to advance it.

I now feel compelled to put into writing the knowledge I have gained about the Lord. My concern is that believers everywhere might know the certainty of those things they have learned. I also intend to write another volume that begins with the Lord's ascension into heaven, relating more fully the acts of the apostles following the advent of the Holy Spirit. My desire is that Christian congregations, whether they be Jew or Gentile, might realize their important role in God's wonderful plan of redemption for this lost world.

✳ ✳ ✳ ✳

Scripture References:

> Colossians 4:14; 2 Timothy 4:11; Philemon 24; the gospel of Luke and the Acts of the Apostles, both written about A.D. 60

Spiritual Reflections:

> Luke was the author of two books, Luke and Acts— approximately one fourth of the New Testament.

> Luke is generally recognized as the most literary writer of the New Testament as well as the first Christian historian. Tradition holds that he was a painter as well.

> Luke's gospel gives greater importance than usual to those not highly esteemed in first century society—women, children, tax collectors, the poor, and outcasts.

Suggested Hymns:

- "My Faith Has Found a Resting Place"
- "Only One Life to Offer"

John ("Beloved Disciple")

Dear children, let us not love with words or tongue but
with actions and in truth (John 3:18).

Somehow the thought of running a large prosperous business
with my father Zebedee (ZEB-e-dee) and my older brother
James never really satisfied my youthful, restless spirit.
Surely, I thought, there must be more to this life than merely
catching and selling fish.

Then one day I heard about a dynamic young preacher
who was attracting a great deal of attention in the desert
region around Jordan. He was known by his many followers
as John the Baptist. My brother and I decided to take some
time off from our fishing business and observe for ourselves
this wilderness preacher who dressed in camel's hair and
ate locusts and wild honey. We were pleased with the
sincerity and forcefulness of this unusual man. We were
also impressed by the large crowds that responded to his
invitations for repentance of sin and were willing to give
witness of conversion by being baptized in the Jordan River.
My first thought was that this preacher was surely the
promised Messiah foretold by the prophets. Yet repeatedly
we heard the Baptizer say that he was not the Christ we
looked for but was simply the voice preparing the way for
this promised One. He told us that the One we were awaiting
was so much greater than himself that he felt unworthy
even to untie His sandals. We pondered these truths carefully
as we returned to our home in Capernaum (ka-PUR-na-um).

Soon after this the Baptizer saw my cousin Jesus of
Nazareth—son of Mary and Joseph, the carpenter—coming
toward him. You can imagine everyone's surprise when the
preacher cried out, "Look, here is the Lamb of God, who
takes away the sin of the world! This is the One I meant
when I said, 'A man who comes after me has surpassed me

because He was before me.' This is the Son of God!" People no doubt were even more surprised when Jesus announced that He too wished to be baptized by John along with the others as a fulfillment of all the requirements of righteousness. As Jesus came up out of the water, the Spirit of God descended upon Him like a dove, and a voice from heaven declared, "You are my Son, whom I love; with You I am well pleased."

One day James and I were busily mending our nets on the shore of Galilee when Jesus came walking toward us. We were quite discouraged just then since we had been fishing all night without success. But seeing Jesus quickly turned our gloom into joy. By this time we were certain that John the Baptist's pronouncement about our cousin was indeed true. Then Jesus spoke words that I will always remember. He invited James and me to leave our fishing business, follow Him, and become fishers of men for God. We left the boats and nets at once and went with Him without as much as a backward glance.

My brother and I became zealous followers of our Master. We worked tirelessly for Him, often becoming impatient and even angry with those we felt were not as devoted as they should be. On one of these occasions, Jesus good-naturedly nicknamed us the "Sons of Thunder" because of our fiery manner.

Only as the days passed, however, did I begin to fully realize something of our Master's great love for people. This was always the very essence of His teaching. How I yearned to be more like Him. Then one day this truth dawned upon me: the very nature of God the Father is love since He had sent His only Son—this very Jesus—into our world in order that we might live eternally with Him. What a demonstration of divine love!

In my closeness with Christ, I often overheard people say, "John is the disciple that Jesus loves." As I continued to experience Christ's love day by day, I felt more and more drawn to Him and anxious to be at His side continually. It seemed that every word He spoke and every story He told had such meaning. And what amazing miracles we saw Him do! People were healed of lifelong diseases, blind eyes were opened, and even dead people were brought back to life.

It became the passion of my life to persuade everyone I met to believe in my Lord and in His message of love. By "believing in Him" I didn't mean simply agreement with what He said, but rather a total surrender of one's life to Him. And it was also my earnest desire that believers in Christ learn to truly love one another even as God demonstrated His love for each of us. Often I have pondered, "How can we say we truly love God and then not love His children?"

In those final days of our Lord's brief time on earth, there were several unforgettable events that stand out in my mind above all the rest: the tragic day when I saw Jesus crucified on that cruel Roman cross and heard Him pray to His Father for the forgiveness of those who had so falsely accused Him; the moment when He looked at His sorrowing mother and then entrusted her lifelong care to me; and, of course, that thrilling Sunday morning when Peter and I stared into the tomb and saw those empty grave clothes. "Our Lord is risen—He is alive!" we shouted to everyone we saw.

Throughout my long lifetime, my conviction about the importance of love has never changed. When my friends ask why I still speak and write so much about this subject, my reply is that this was our Lord's foremost command. If we fulfill this, nothing more is needed. Let me say it one more time so that no one will fail to understand: "This is love . . . not that we loved God, but that He loved us and sent His Son as an atoning sacrifice for our sins. Dear friends, since God so loved us . . . we also ought to love one another."

❋ ❋ ❋ ❋

Scripture References:
> Matthew 3:1–12; 4:21; Mark 1:1–9; 3:17; John 1:29–39; 13:23; 19:26–27; 20:2–8; 1 John 4:10–11

Spiritual Reflections:
> Author of the gospel of John, the three epistles of John, and the Revelation, all written around A.D. 85–95.

John and his brother James were among the first disciples called by Jesus. Along with Peter, these three formed an inner circle of disciples closest to the Lord.

"Let there be in the essentials, UNITY. In all non-essentials, LIBERTY. In all things, CHARITY (love)."
—Augustine

"No amount of truth in the head replaces a lack of God's love in the heart."   —author unknown

"Love is simply Christianity in action."
—author unknown

"As Christians we should always work heart-to-heart even though we do not always see things eye-to-eye."
—author unknown

Suggested Hymns:
- "O the Deep, Deep Love of Jesus"
- "Just a Closer Walk with Thee"

Elizabeth

All the ends of the earth will see the salvation of our
God (Isaiah 52:10).

I should have been content with my privileged life as the
wife of a priest, but my heart was sorrowful, for I had no
children and we were no longer young. My husband
Zacharias (ZAK-a-RI-as) and I are both descendants of Aaron,
the brother of Moses. We live in ancient Hebron (HE-bron),
the city of the priests, where Father Abraham and his family
are buried. We had always been diligent in observing the
commandments of Jehovah and in following His leading in
our lives. Yet our fervent prayers for a child were still
unanswered.

Another of our continual prayers has been for the coming
of our promised Messiah. Malachi foretold in the Scriptures
that the Sun of Righteousness would rise with healing in
His wings, and just before His coming a prophet would
appear to prepare Israel for their Redeemer. But four hundred
silent years have passed since Malachi's prophecy. Our
people have been persecuted by many nations and are now
suffering under cruel Roman rule. Our temple has been
desecrated and our corrupt religious leaders have
disillusioned us. How our hearts have yearned for God's
promised Deliverer.

Then one Sabbath as the priests were casting lots for the
special privilege of offering the burnt incense in the Holy
Place of the temple, my husband Zacharias was the one
chosen. As he approached the golden altar, he was startled
by a brilliant light! An angel addressed him, "Do not be
afraid, Zacharias. Your wife Elizabeth will bear a son and
you are to give him the name John. He will be a joy and
delight to you, and many will rejoice because of his birth.
He will be great in the sight of the Lord. Many of the people

117

of Israel will he bring back to the Lord their God . . . to make ready a people prepared for their Redeemer."

Zacharias was astonished . . . and doubtful because of our advanced ages. The angel rebuked him. "I am Gabriel . . . I stand in the presence of God and I have been sent to speak to you and tell you this good news. But because you doubted my words, which will come true at their proper time, you will be silent and unable to speak until that day occurs!"

Confused and fearful, Zacharias hastened to convey to me, in writing, the message of the angel. I was amazed for now the promise of a forerunner of God's anointed Messiah would be fulfilled at last. I was overjoyed for I knew that nothing is impossible with God! I had always known that my name Elizabeth means "God's promise!" . . . and I praised my Lord for His faithfulness and covenant of love. He had shown me great mercy and had taken away my disgrace of barrenness among the people.

I spent much time in prayer and worship as I quietly awaited the birth of my son. Then in the sixth month I received news that my relative Mary, a young maiden from the obscure little village of Nazareth, planned to visit and rejoice with us. When I greeted her upon her arrival, suddenly the babe leaped for joy within me. Then the wonderful truth was revealed to me. "Blessed are you among women," I cried, "and blessed is the child you will bear! But why am I so favored that the mother of my Lord should come to me?"

Mary responded: "The angel Gabriel appeared to me saying, 'You will give birth to a son and you are to call Him Jesus. The Lord God will give Him the throne of His Father David and He will reign over the house of Jacob forever. His kingdom will never end!'" As we rejoiced and praised God together, I exclaimed, "Blessed is she who has believed that what the Lord has said to her will be accomplished!"

And it surely was!

Scripture References:
    Luke 1:5–25; 39–45; Malachi 4:2

Spiritual Reflections:

It has often been said that whenever God reveals Himself to a person, He always confirms that message through circumstances or the witness of another individual. Note how this was true with Elizabeth and Mary as well as throughout the entire account of Jesus' advent.

"Rejoice! rejoice! Emmanuel shall come to thee, O Israel."
—12th century

Suggested Hymns:
- "O Come, O Come, Emmanuel"
- "That Beautiful Name"

Drama 32

Simeon (SIM-e-un)

> Arise, shine; for your light has come, and the glory of
> the Lord has risen upon you (Isaiah 60:1 NAS).

I unrolled the sheepskin scroll carefully and read the sacred words of Isaiah once again, "And the glory of the Lord will be revealed, and all mankind together will see it. For the mouth of the Lord has spoken!" I began to muse about how our Jewish people have been waiting earnestly now for centuries for our promised Messiah to be born. We knew from the Scriptures that He would come from the line of our Father David and would deliver us from the hands of our many enemies. How our hearts yearned for this Holy One to appear.

I will never forget one wonderful day when I was still a very young man. God's Spirit came upon me with the thrilling promise that I would not leave this life until my very eyes had seen the anointed Comforter of Israel, the Lord's Christ. Imagine me, Simeon, just a humble Jewish citizen of this vast city of Jerusalem, receiving such a message from Jehovah Himself. I was filled with awe! This hope filled my long life with love and praise for God as I humbly tried to worship and serve Him.

Each day I have gone to our nearby Temple, not only to worship but also to discover if the secret that God placed in my heart had come true. I was confident that in the fullness of time the Sun of Righteousness would appear to redeem us from our sinful state. With a sigh, I put away the precious scroll and made my way eagerly toward the Temple courts for my daily visit. I was awed as usual at the sight of the beautiful golden roof and the marble steps before me. As I walked through the sacred place and knelt to pray, I was filled with a special awareness of God's nearness. My heart was stirred with deep gratefulness for His love and mercy to me.

After a time I rose and began to move quietly through the wide doors. Coming toward me just then was a young mother with an infant in her arms. She looked so serene and joyful that I stopped to look more carefully at her. She was accompanied by an older looking man, who appeared patient and kind. They were carrying a cage with two small doves to be sacrificed as part of our Jewish consecration service for a first-born son. As they moved toward the altar with the offering, I could clearly see the baby. I was startled. What a peaceful and beautiful expression on that little face. I began to tremble, for there was that still small voice of God within me once again. Surely this must be the promised One! Hastening toward the parents, I heard them tell nearby onlookers that their baby's name was Jesus. Then they proudly showed their son to me and I reached out timidly to take Him. At last—I was holding God's promised Messiah in my own arms! Out of a joyous heart my praise began: "Oh Sovereign Lord, as You have promised, You may now dismiss Your servant in peace, for my eyes have seen Your salvation, which You have prepared in the sight of all people, a light of revelation to the Gentiles, and the glory of Your people Israel."

The parents were astonished and pleased to hear me speaking such prophetic words about their son. Then the Lord's Spirit gave me these words of blessing for them: "This Child is destined to cause the falling and rising of many in Israel . . . so that the thoughts of many hearts will be revealed."

But as I returned the Child to His young mother, sadness overwhelmed me. I felt God's Spirit upon me once again, moving me to tell her that because of this Child, grief would one day come upon her, like a sharp sword piercing her very soul.

As I was about to leave, the prophetess Anna came over to join us. She was one of the elderly women who ministered faithfully in the Temple and for her lifelong devotion to God was highly respected by all. It had also been revealed to her that this Child was the Redeemer of Israel. Together we began praising Jehovah, our covenant keeping God, who had been faithful to His eternal promise. Messiah had come!

✻ ✻ ✻ ✻

Scripture References:
Isaiah 40:5; Luke 2:21–38

Spiritual Reflections:

> This, this is Christ the King,
>   whom shepherds guard and angels sing;
> Haste, haste to bring Him laud,
>   the babe, the son of Mary!
> —William C. Dix

Simeon, "a righteous and devout man," was the first to recognize Jesus as Israel's promised Messiah and the redeemer of the gentiles as well. His prayer has become one of the beloved hymn texts of the church. Its name, the "Nunc Dimittis," is taken from the first two Latin words in the phrase "Lord, now lettest Thy servant depart in peace . . ."

Suggested Hymns:
- "Come, Thou Long-Expected Jesus"
- "What Child Is This?"

Peter

Lord, to whom shall we go? You have the words of
eternal life (John 6:68).

"Who do people say the Son of Man is?" One day the Lord
posed this searching question to us. We twelve disciples
had been ministering to the people in the region of Caesarea
(SES-a-RE-ah) and had returned at the end of a busy day to
share our experiences with the Master and with each other.
It seemed odd that Jesus sensed immediately that His identity
was the foremost question everyone was asking about Him.

One by one my fellow disciples began responding. They
told Jesus that many people thought He was really John the
Baptist or possibly Elijah. Others were convinced that He
was Jeremiah or one of the other prophets returned from the
dead. There was a moment of silence as our Lord looked
directly at each of us before speaking again. "But what about
you? Who do you say I am?"

I felt the gaze of the others focused on me as they awaited
my reply. Without hesitation I spoke out firmly, "You are
the Christ, the Son of the Living God." Jesus seemed
especially pleased with my answer. He stated that this was
the very truth upon which He would build His church and
expand His earthly kingdom throughout the world.

As I now reflect upon those three wonderful years spent
with our Lord, it seems almost impossible to recall all of
the lessons and the miracles we shared with Him. There
is, however, one unforgettable event that I will always
cherish.

One evening our Lord had just told the twelve of us to get
into a boat and sail for the other side of the lake. We were
scarcely on our way before the wind and water became
wildly turbulent. As the night grew blacker, we were
increasingly fearful. Adding to our fright was the sight of a

shadowy figure walking on the water. "It's a ghost!" we cried out in horror.

Then the calm voice of our Master rose above the howling wind. "Take courage, friends, it is I. Don't be afraid!"

I was so excited and relieved at seeing the Lord that I shouted out, "Master, tell me to come to You on the water."

"Come," He beckoned.

Immediately I climbed out of the boat nervously and began walking slowly toward Him. What a thrilling experience! But a strong wind whipped up, splashing a huge wave over me. I panicked and started to sink. "Lord, save me!"

I felt the strong grasp of the Lord's hand on mine. When He helped me into the boat, He smiled at me compassionately. "Peter, your faith is too small. You must learn to trust Me more completely." As He stepped into our boat, instantly the wind ceased and the water became calm. We disciples were so awed that we dropped to our knees in worship, reaffirming our faith in His deity by exclaiming in hushed tones, "Truly You are the Son of God!"

Another experience with Jesus I will always remember . . . but with great regret. It was, no doubt, the most shameful and darkest day of my entire life. After sharing the Passover Supper with the Lord, we all went to the Mount of Olives. There the Master quoted an Old Testament Scripture to us, foretelling that the Shepherd would be smitten and His sheep scattered. Although I didn't understand fully the meaning of the passage, I sensed that the Lord was trying to teach us something important. I blurted out quickly that even if every person in the world would fall away, I for one certainly would not. "Even if I have to die with You, I will never disown You!" And the other disciples readily agreed.

After this we went to the Garden of Gethsemane, where our Lord told us to watch and wait while He went farther on and prayed alone. It was dark and lonely there as the hours passed slowly. Three times the Master returned and found us sleeping. Then Judas, who had left earlier during the Passover Supper, suddenly appeared in the darkness with a noisy crowd of people armed with swords and clubs. As Judas embraced the Master, the wild and hysterical mob seized our Lord forcibly and dragged Him to the high priest, accusing Jesus of blasphemy that made Him guilty of death. Almost paralyzed with fear, I watched from a distance as the scene unfolded. The Master was blindfolded, spit upon, struck with fists, and taunted by those vicious people.

I was devastated! Were those past three years with Jesus all in vain? Stricken and confused, I saw a nearby fire where some of the guards were warming themselves. Making my way there, I joined them to relieve my shivering. Just then a little servant girl came by, pointed her finger at me and sneered, "You were with that Nazarene, Jesus."

"I don't know or understand what you're talking about," I muttered softly and retreated into the entryway. Later when the same girl passed me, she again pointed her finger mockingly at me and told those standing around that I was one of Jesus' followers. I spoke out loudly this time so that everyone could hear. "You are all completely wrong!"

Then some of the soldiers came by and taunted me. "Surely you are one of them. You must be . . . for you are a Galilean." This time, I shouted out with vile words that I hadn't used for three years, "I do not know this man of whom you speak!" Like a bugle call I heard a rooster crow . . . and I recalled with shame the words of my Lord spoken earlier that evening when I was being so boastful. "Before the cock crows twice, Peter, you will disown Me three times." With bitter tears I stumbled and crouched against a wall. Though broken and remorseful, I sensed in my spirit that my blessed Lord would understand and forgive.

How quickly the events of the next few weeks passed. After our Lord's cruel death there was His glorious resurrection. Then came His wonderful final days with us, His thrilling ascension into heaven, and finally the advent of the Holy Spirit. I felt a new devotion to my Lord and a fervent desire to proclaim His message to everyone. Daily we saw great crowds of people repent of their sins and believe in Christ. They were baptized in His name and added to the fellowship of believers.

As I now approach the end of my life, I realize increasingly that if believers are to live steadfast spiritual lives, each day must be a time of growth in the grace and knowledge of our Lord. To our initial faith in Christ we must make every effort to add such virtues as goodness, self-control, perseverance, godliness, brotherly kindness, and above all else—love! And then, my dear brothers and sisters, let us learn to cast all of our concerns and anxieties upon the Lord, knowing with certainty that He truly cares for each of us.

❊ ❊ ❊ ❊

Scripture References:
Matthew 14:22–32; 16:13–20; Mark 6:45–52; Luke 22:54–62; Acts 2: and 1 and 2 Peter, written about A.D. 65–66.

Spiritual Reflections:
Consider how Peter, such an unlikely candidate, could become the most prominent of Jesus' disciples as well as the leader and spokesman for the early Christian church.

It is believed that Peter was martyred about the same time as the apostle Paul, A.D. 67 or 68, during the persecution of the Christians by the Roman Emperor Nero. Tradition states that Peter felt himself to be unworthy to die in the same manner as his Master and was therefore, at his own request, crucified with his head downward.

Suggested Hymns:
- "In the Hour of Trial"
- "I Am His and He Is Mine"

Philip

Any of you who does not give up everything he has cannot be My disciple (Luke 14:33).

I remember well the day Jesus visited our little fishing town of Bethsaida (BETH-SA i-dah) on the northern shore of Lake Galilee. He sought me out and in a straightforward manner invited me to follow Him. For some time I had heard of this teacher from Nazareth and His amazing ministry throughout the region. He, no doubt, also had heard of me from His recent followers, two brothers from our town—Andrew and Peter. They knew that I had been a serious student of the Old Testament writings. I was a fervent believer that one day a Messiah would be born who would establish a new kingdom of peace and justice. How I had prayed for this to occur.

As strange as it may seem, when Jesus invited me to follow Him, I immediately left everything behind and went with Him. This kind of impulsive behavior is so unlike me. I have always had an inquiring mind and am normally most careful about every detail before making any decision, but I sensed in my spirit that I had truly found that for which I had been longing.

In fact, I was so enthusiastic about this encounter with Jesus that I ran to the nearby home of my friend Nathanael, who also was much interested in the coming of Messiah. He and I have had many long discussions about this matter. "Nathanael," I cried out, "we have found the One Moses wrote about in the Law and about whom the prophets also spoke—Jesus of Nazareth, the son of Joseph."

But Nathanael was skeptical. "Nazareth!" he sneered, "Can anything good come from there?"

"Just come and see for yourself," I pleaded.

When Jesus saw Nathanael approaching, He said kindly, "Here is a true Israelite, in whom there is nothing false."

Nathanael was overcome with this greeting. "How do you know me?" he stammered.

Jesus answered him calmly, "I saw you while you were still under the fig tree before Philip called you." Nathanael's skepticism quickly disappeared.

From that day on, Nathanael and I became zealous followers of our Lord. We listened carefully to His teachings and marveled at the wonders He performed, like the miracle in Cana when He changed water into choice wine. As time went on, more and more people saw these miraculous signs and became followers of the Master and His little band of disciples.

One day just before the time of the busy Jewish Passover, Jesus took the twelve of us to a mountainside for a time of rest and learning. While we were seated there, we noticed that a large crowd of people had also gathered to hear the Master. I thought Jesus surely would send them away since it was now time for our evening meal. But without warning, He turned to me and asked, "Philip, where shall we buy bread for these people to eat?"

I pondered His question carefully. Could Jesus really be serious? Didn't He realize that we twelve disciples would have to labor at least eight months to provide even bread for this many people? Then I noticed Andrew approaching a young boy carrying a basket of food. "Here is a lad with five small barley loaves and two little fish," Andrew called to Jesus, "but how far will that go with so many?" Calmly the Lord told us to have everyone take a seat on the grass. And what a crowd there was—at least five thousand men alone! We were puzzled as we watched Jesus take the boy's food and give thanks. He directed us to begin distributing it, making sure that everyone had enough. When they had finished, the Lord told us to gather up the pieces that remained so that nothing would be wasted. And can you believe that when everything was finally collected, there were twelve full baskets of food left over from merely those five barley loaves and two little fish!

When the people realized the miraculous event that had just occurred, they began murmuring among themselves that Jesus surely was the long-awaited Prophet about whom the

Scriptures foretold. Some of them even began chanting that now was the time to make Him their king. But the Lord quietly removed Himself from the crowd and went alone to another part of the mountain.

The next several years were truly wonderful as we traveled around with our Master. We learned so much from Him. He taught us about living an abundant life, about praying to our heavenly Father, and about preparing for eternity. However, there was always one underlying truth that I could never fully grasp. How could Jesus and God the Father be the same person?

There came the time when the Jewish religious leaders began revolting against our Master. They told the people that Jesus was a blasphemer by claiming that He was the Son of God. Our Lord had warned us, however, that this must occur . . . that He would be put to death but would rise again and then return to His Father in heaven. One day as we were discussing these matters, I finally blurted out my long-time concern . . . "Lord, show us the Father and that will be enough for us."

Jesus fixed His gaze on me as He rebuked me firmly but with compassion. "Don't you know Me, Philip, even after I have been among you such a long time? Anyone who has seen Me has seen the Father. How can you say, 'Show us the Father?' Don't you believe that I am in the Father, and that the Father is in Me? The words I say to you are not just My own. Rather, it is the Father, living in Me, who is doing His work."

Our Lord was crucified and rose from the grave just as He had foretold. Then for forty unforgettable days after His resurrection, He showed Himself to us as well as to many of His other followers. Any doubts that we might have had regarding His deity had by then completely vanished. On one occasion while we were sharing a meal together, the Lord announced that we were to remain here in Jerusalem to await the promised gift of the Holy Spirit. After that we would be empowered to take His transforming message to the very ends of the earth.

At last the day came when we went with the Master to the nearby Mount of Olives. As we stood there together, He was suddenly taken up before our very eyes! We stared into the sky with astonishment! Then two men dressed in white stood beside us and proclaimed, "This same Jesus will one day return in the same way you have seen Him go into heaven."

Filled with praise and worship, we returned to Jerusalem to await the gift of the Holy Spirit. We were eager to begin our mission of sharing with everyone the glorious message of the Master—our risen, victorious Lord and coming King!

✳ ✳ ✳ ✳

Scripture References:
   Mark 6:32–44; John 1:43–51; 6:1–15; 14:8–12; Acts 1:3–14

Spiritual Reflections:
   Tradition states that Philip preached and died in Asia Minor. In later centuries, legends concerning the apostle Philip were compiled in a volume titled *The Acts of Philip.* However, in this work he was often confused with Philip the evangelist, a leader of the Jerusalem church in its early days.

   The twelve disciples called by Jesus: Andrew, Philip, Nathanael, Matthew, Simon, James (the unknown), Judas (Thaddaeus), Judas Iscariot, Peter, James, John, Thomas. (Matt. 10:2–4; Mark 3:16–19; Luke 6:14–16; Acts 1:13)

   "Salvation is free, but discipleship is costly."
                                           —anonymous

Suggested Hymns:
   • "I Have Decided to Follow Jesus"
   • "Breathe on Me, Breath of God"

Thomas

When my heart is overwhelmed, lead me to the Rock
that is higher than I (Psalm 61:2 KJV).

I must confess that I was always a rather anxious person,
often becoming despondent and gloomy. But since knowing
Jesus, I had such great hopes for our Master and His eternal
kingdom. How dearly I loved Him and believed His
promises with all my heart. Then suddenly came those days
of tragedy . . . the betrayal, the arrest, and the heart-rending
crucifixion. I was filled with despair. My whole world
collapsed, and I was overcome with confusion and grief.
My days were spent in darkness and brooding, avoiding
even my fellow disciples.

What could be the meaning of all this? We had trusted so
implicitly in the glorious truths our Lord taught us. We had
such visions of a better world, a kingdom of love and joy
where life would have real meaning. But then He was gone,
and there seemed to be no future left. My tears flowed as I
recalled our great expectations while Jesus was with us. Was
it all in vain?

I wandered around aimlessly for several days thinking
my fellow disciples would not care to see me. I had never
been cheerful and exuberant like Peter and the others, so
what comfort could I be to them now? The crucifixion was
like a deathblow to all of us . . . how deeply we had loved
Him!

I tried to remember some of those unusual truths the
Master had taught us. "In a little while you will see Me no
more . . . and then after a little while you will see Me." We
had looked vaguely at each other, whispering, "We don't
understand what He is saying." On another occasion we
questioned, "Lord, we know not where You are going . . .
and how can we know the way?" Jesus explained to us that

He was the way, and each person must come to the Father through Him.

Several days passed before I began to feel that I should seek out the other disciples to see if they were still safe. Perhaps we could comfort each other by recalling some of the memorable experiences we had shared with our Lord. After much inquiry I learned of their secret location from one of the women who had also followed the Master. To find them I had to creep silently along a deserted street at night. I made my way up a back stairway of the room where the disciples were gathered. I was startled by the sounds of a joyous but muted excitement. After my knock someone pulled me quickly through the door and whispered, "Thomas, we have seen the Lord!" I was stunned! Were they having delusions? I stared at them in disbelief. Had some imposter tricked them? I could not believe they were telling me the truth. I had stood there at the cross witnessing with my own tear-filled eyes the cruel execution of Jesus. How could it be possible that He was alive again? I was certain that their minds had been affected by much sorrow. After a moment I blurted out, "Unless I see the nail marks in His hands and put my hand into His side, I will not believe it!" As they stood silently staring at me, I stumbled out the door.

My sad and pessimistic state of mind stayed with me all through the following week. Then I heard that the others were planning to meet again in the same secret location. I decided to join them. After everyone had arrived, we kept our voices low and made certain that the doors were secure. We were still fearful of the Jewish leaders. Suddenly in the midst of our conversation there was a hushed silence. Jesus stood before us, smiling and saying, "Peace be with you!" I stared at Him in unbelief. Yet truly it was Jesus just as I knew Him. I stood speechless, but at once He moved closer to me, saying gently, "Put your finger here; see my hands. Reach out your hand and put it into my side." Then looking directly into my eyes, he said, "Stop doubting, Thomas, and believe!"

"My Lord and my God!" I fell to my knees in humble adoration before Him.

"Because you have seen Me," Jesus continued, "you have believed. Blessed are those who have not seen and yet have believed."

My bent for doubting has been replaced with a new spirit of praise and devotion for Christ, our ever-living Lord and Master. My remaining days will be spent in sharing His glorious truths with others.

❋ ❋ ❋

Scripture References:
    John 11:16; 14:4–6; 20:24–29; Acts 1:13

Spiritual Reflections:
    Tradition states that Thomas later ministered in Persia and possibly in India.

    "There is often more faith in honest doubt than in the glib recitation of our religious creeds."
                                    —paraphrase of Tennyson

    "The best way to starve an honest doubt is to feed it a daily diet of fresh faith."   —author unknown

    "To any soul who honestly seeks for truth, Christ will always reveal Himself" (see Jer. 29:13).
                                    —author unknown

Suggested Hymns:
    • "Near to the Heart of God"
    • "Jesus, I Am Resting"

Drama 36

Zacchaeus (za-KE-us)

No servant can serve two masters . . . you cannot serve
both God and money (Luke 16:13).

The cheering and exuberance of a crowd caught my attention.
I ran eagerly toward the gathering to see what could be
happening. Stopping to rest a moment, I stood on a rock to
look ahead, but I was much too short to see over those
around me. "Who is it?" I called to someone.

"Why it's that prophet from Nazareth called Jesus," they
shouted. "Haven't you heard about Him?"

I was curious. What kind of man could create such a stir? I
ran ahead of the crowd, straining to see better. Even the window
ledges and rooftops were already filled with people. I dashed
on until I saw a sturdy Sycamore tree nearby. Breathless by
this time, I managed to pull myself up to the lowest branch just
as the mysterious prophet approached. People shoved each
other and clamored around Him, many calling out for His
help. Several of His helpers were having a difficult time clearing
a path for Him. But the prophet remained calm, with such a
kind expression on His face . . . in spite of all the confusion. I
could see Him clearly as He moved along until He was directly
under my tree. To my amazement, He stopped abruptly, looked
up at me and called my name—"Zacchaeus." I was startled!
How could He possibly know my name . . . this man that I had
never seen before? "Zacchaeus, come down immediately," He
called out. "I must stay at your house today." Almost tumbling
from the tree, I smoothed out my clothing nervously and began
leading the way to my home.

As we walked along I turned occasionally to look at the
crowd. Many had now drawn away from us. Others pointed
their fingers at us with sneers. I could hear them murmuring,
"Can you believe that Jesus will be the guest of a sinner?" I
knew I was commonly hated and often called a sinner

because I was a tax collector for the Romans. My duty was to oversee the tributes that our Hebrew people must pay the government. Since they thought that I often demanded more payment than they really owed, the Jewish people no longer considered me to be one of their own. Rather they looked upon me as a traitor and a friend of the hated Romans.

Perhaps I had been overly ambitious in seeking a position of power when I reached manhood. Possibly this was because I had never received much acceptance when I was young. I had always been short in stature, and my playmates taunted me with such comments as, "Isn't that little Zacchaeus ever going to grow up?" My greatest desire as I grew older was to be admired and accepted. With hard work I reached the high position of chief tax collector for the entire region of Jericho. Although the job paid well and made me quite wealthy, my luxurious home and comfortable life-style had not made me happy. With little true friendship in life, I felt increasingly restless and lonely. But now even with the jeers of the crowd behind us, this gracious stranger continued to walk beside me calmly as I led the way to my home.

It was truly the most wonderful day in my entire life. As Jesus visited with us, His teachings pierced through my heart. He made me aware of my greed and dishonesty and the shallow pride and ambition that made me put a desire for recognition above the love for my people. I was ashamed and repentant that I had used my position to treat others unjustly. With love and compassion Jesus revealed a better way of life that would be mine if I simply trusted Him and followed His teachings. No one had ever before made me feel so worthwhile. As I sat at His feet listening for hours, I was filled with remorse and a deep desire to please Him. "Lord, Lord," I exclaimed as I rose to my feet, "here and now I will give half of my possessions to the poor. If I have cheated anybody out of anything, I will pay back four times the amount!"

Jesus gazed at me for a moment with loving approval. Then turning to the others who had gathered outside my home, He declared, "Today salvation has come to this house because this man, too, is a Son of Abraham." There were still some self-righteous people in the crowd who were openly critical of Jesus' action. The Master rebuked them by calmly stating, "The Son of Man came to seek and to save what was lost."

I knew for certain that Jesus had given me a changed heart. At last I felt that I was truly loved and forgiven . . . a Jewish person of genuine worth. It no longer mattered that I was small!

✹✹✹✹

Scripture Reference:
   Luke 19:1–10

Spiritual Reflections:
   This story illustrates the truth that sinners who display a truly penitent attitude are more worthy of Christ's forgiveness than persons pretending to be pious. A broken heart is the first step to spiritual wholeness.

   "All my theology is reduced to this narrow compass—Christ Jesus came into this world to save sinners."
                                        —Archibald Alexander

   He became poor that we might become rich (James 2:5).
   He was born that we might be born again (John 1:14).
   He became a servant that we might become sons (Gal. 4:6–7).
   He had no home that we might have a mansion in heaven (Matt. 8:20).
   He was bound that we might go free (John 8:32–36).
   He was made sin that we might be made righteous (2 Cor. 5:21).
   He died that we might live eternally (John 5:24–25).

Come, ye sinners, poor and needy,
weak and wounded, sick and sore,
Jesus ready stands to save you,
full of pity, love and pow'r.

Let not conscience make you linger,
nor of fitness fondly dream.
All the fitness He requireth
is to feel your need of Him.

Come, ye weary, heavy laden,
bruis'd and mangled by the fall;
If you tarry till you're better,
you will never come at all.

—Joseph Hart

In the home Christianity is kindness;
In business it is honesty
In society it is helpfulness;
Toward the unfortunate it is the helping hand;
Toward the sinner it is evangelism;
Toward the erring it is forgiveness;
Toward ourselves it is self-control;
Toward God it is worship, love and service.

—author unknown

Suggested Hymns:
- "Jesus, What a Friend of Sinners!"
- "Higher Ground"

Drama 37

Nicodemus (NIK-o-DE-mus)

And you will seek Me and find Me when you search
for Me with all your heart (Jer. 29:13 NAS).

How dark it was and rough underfoot. I stumbled and
groped my way along the mountain path, peering ahead in
the black mist. Perhaps I had been foolish to arrange this
meeting in such secrecy. But I was curious about the man
called Jesus of Nazareth and knew I must be cautious. To be
seen with Him in public would be harmful to my reputation
as a devoted and honored member of the Sanhedrin (SAN-
he-drin), the ruling council of our temple. My fellow priests
would certainly ridicule me if they knew I was seeking out
this unknown prophet. And He was always so pressed with
crowds around Him during the day that it would be difficult
to speak with Him alone. Privately I made plans to meet
Him in this secluded place at night.

As I made my way, I continued to ponder who this man
from Galilee really might be. Since I was a leader of our
Jewish people, I had been well instructed in the Holy
Scriptures and was always one of those sent to investigate
whenever teachers of suspected heresy appeared. We had
already questioned John the Baptist—"Are you God's
Promised Prophet?" We were puzzled with his denials. Then
we began hearing about this new teacher from Nazareth.
Reports kept coming to us that great crowds followed Him
everywhere. They reported that He healed the sick, cured
the blind, and even raised the dead. His teachings also
alarmed us for He promised the forgiveness of sin, criticized
our honored traditions, and openly condemned our priestly
leadership. To try to learn more about this stranger, my
fellow priests and I would blend with the crowds whenever
we could.

Who is He, I kept pondering? Is He a blasphemer or merely

a clever deceiver? Perhaps He is a self-deluded prophet who feels He must warn us of our sins and hypocrisy. Yet so many of our good people say they have been helped by Him and believe that He was truly sent from God. And if this were true, I would not really dare to oppose Him. I felt increasingly compelled to talk with Jesus alone . . . to learn more about this unusual man. Yet because of my standing in the community, it had to be a secret meeting at night.

My thoughts were interrupted by the dim outline of Jesus sitting quietly on a rock just ahead of me. As soon as we had greeted each other, I began, "Rabbi, we know you are a teacher who has come from God. Truly no one could perform the miraculous signs you are doing if God were not with him."

I was startled by His direct reply. "I tell you the truth, Nicodemus, unless a man is born of water and the Spirit, he cannot enter God's kingdom." Had Jesus read my thoughts? I had spent much time lately pondering the matter of when the kingdom of Israel would be restored.

"How can a man be born anew when he is old?" I asked him. "Surely he cannot enter a second time into his mother's womb to be born!"

Jesus responded patiently, "The wind blows wherever it pleases. You hear its sound but cannot tell where it comes from or where it is going. So it is with everyone born of the Spirit. You are Israel's teacher and do not understand these things? I have spoken to you of earthly things and you do not believe; how then will you believe if I speak of heavenly things? Just as Moses lifted up the snake in the desert, so the Son of Man must be lifted up, that everyone who believes in Him may have eternal life."

After I went my way, the searching words of Jesus were etched in my mind. I was well enough acquainted with the Old Testament to recall the words of Ezekiel about life renewed by the breath of God's Spirit in answer to a prayer of faith. I knew that this is the way man is born to eternal life. From that time on I tried whenever possible to join the crowds around Jesus to hear His teachings. The more I listened the more convinced I became that He spoke the truth and could indeed be the Holy One sent from God.

One day as the crowd thronged around the Master, I stood nearby with my fellow priests. They began to deride Jesus, saying, "Has any of the rulers of the Pharisees believed in Him? No! But this mob that knows nothing of the law . . . there is a curse on them."

Their hateful statements troubled me. I knew I must be careful of defending the Master openly, yet I felt compelled to say something favorable. I asked, "Does our law condemn a man without first hearing Him to find out what He is doing?"

Angrily they confronted me. "Are you from Galilee too? Look into it, Nicodemus, and you will find that a prophet does not come out of Galilee." Somehow their opposition made me even more anxious to discover all I could about Jesus. Finally, I determined in my heart to be one of His faithful followers. I grew increasingly bold in my association with His friends and the disciples.

How anguished I felt during those devastating days of Jesus' trial and crucifixion. I stood openly grieving with His other followers beneath the dreadful cross. Once again the prophetic words of that dark night came to me. "Just as Moses lifted up the snake in the wilderness . . . " His teachings were now very clear to me.

After the final hours of Jesus' agony, Joseph of Arimathea (AR i-ma-THE-ah), a God-fearing man, received permission to care for the burial. As our Master was carried to a new tomb in the garden near the hill of Calvary, Joseph and I followed along. Lovingly we wrapped His body in linens, embalming it with a costly mixture of ointments. I returned to my home with a grieving heart.

And then that thrilling Sunday morning—what unspeakable joy. Our Lord had risen! With awe and wonder we listened to the reports from those who had actually seen and spoken with Him. "Jesus is alive" were the words on every believer's lips.

My secret meeting with Jesus and His words of truth on that dark night will remain with me forever. They guide me even now to true faith and the worship of my living Lord.

* * * *

Scripture References:
   John 1:20–28; 3:1–16, 25–53; 7:51–52; 19:39–42

Spiritual Reflections:
   "You will know the truth, and the truth will set you free" (John 8:32).

> Come dry your tears, you sons of men—
> The Lord's not dead, but risen!
> The mighty stone is rolled away
> From death's cold, gloomy prison.
> Hear how He calls you by your name!
> Behold, the empty prison!
> Run! send the tidings to all men—
> The Lord indeed is risen!
> > —author unknown

Suggested Hymns:
   • "Ye Must Be Born Again"
   • "Because He Lives"

Drama 38

Martha

O Lord, You are my God; I will exalt You and praise Your name, for . . . You have done marvelous things (Isaiah 25:1).

The day was hot, and I was rushed and nervous with all the preparations of a special meal to honor Jesus. He and His disciples had come to rest awhile as they were passing through our village of Bethany. It had been another busy day among the surging crowds that followed them. As I paused for a moment to wipe my flushed face, I noticed that my sister Mary, who shared our home, was no longer helping me. Then I saw her sitting at the feet of Jesus, listening intently to what He was saying. I became irritated. Couldn't Jesus understand how much I had to do in order to prepare a fine meal for everyone? Finally, I exclaimed indignantly, "Lord, don't You care at all that my sister sits here and lets me do all the work alone? Would You tell her to help me?"

There was a pause in the conversation. Then Jesus turned to look directly at me. Rather than a look of rebuke, however, there was kindness and sympathy in His eyes. Soothingly He answered, "Martha, you are worried and upset about many things, but only one thing is needed. Mary has chosen what is better, and it will not be taken away from her."

Silently I returned to my duties in the kitchen. I pondered His words. At times it seemed difficult to understand the meaning of what He said. Had I been so busily engaged in doing things for Him . . . trying to please Him with my activity . . . that I had not taken time to listen closely to His teachings? Even though it was not our custom for women to sit talking with men, Mary was so devoted to Jesus that she always listened attentively and asked discerning questions of Him.

I began to realize that I had not given Jesus the kind of

attention He deserved. My many household duties as well as pride in my accomplishments had kept me from hearing many of the truths the Master had wanted to reveal to us.

After that day I tried to spend more time near Him, and I listened carefully to His teachings. I also became deeply moved by the miraculous deeds we saw Him do. Jesus became our most valued friend. Often we heard Him say that He is God's Son, and we began to understand the truth of His words when He told us, "The Father is in Me and I in the Father." My heart was filled with awe at the realization that Jesus is truly the promised Messiah living among us!

Then one day our brother Lazarus, who loved Jesus dearly, became very ill. We knew that our Lord was presently across the Jordan River teaching the many people in that region. Although we immediately sent word about our brother's illness, we heard nothing from Jesus. And in spite of our best care, Lazarus died. Our grief was indescribable, even though our friends and relatives came to console us. Adding to our grief was the realization that Jesus had not cared enough to come to us. We had been so sure that He truly loved us and would have been able to help.

Four days after the burial of Lazarus, a friend burst into our home to tell me that Jesus had arrived and was waiting at the edge of the village. As quickly as I could I hurried to meet Him. Upon seeing Him, I cried out, "Lord, if You had been here, my brother would not have died."

Calmly Jesus answered, "Your brother will rise again."

"I know he will rise again in the last day," I replied.

"Martha, I am the resurrection and the life. He who believes in Me will live, even though he dies, and whoever lives and believes in Me will never die. Do you believe this?"

His eyes searched mine as I hesitated briefly before responding, "Yes, Lord, I believe that You are the Christ, the Son of God, who was to come into the world!"

I hastened home to bring Mary to Jesus. Upon seeing Him, she fell at His feet, weeping. Then Jesus also wept.

"Where have you laid him?" the Master asked. With the other mourners following, we led Him to the burial cave, which had a stone across the entrance. Jesus commanded, "Take away the stone!"

"But, Lord," I quickly protested, "by this time there is a bad odor, for he has been there four days."

Then His words rang out for all to hear. "Did I not tell you that if you believed, you would see the glory of God?" And as the men rolled away the heavy stone, Jesus looked up to heaven. "Father, I thank You that You have heard Me. I know that You always hear Me, but I said this for the benefit of the people standing here, that they may believe that You sent me. LAZARUS, COME OUT!"

There was a hushed silence as all eyes were fixed on the tomb. And my brother came out . . . with his hands and feet bound and a burial napkin still around his face. What a day of rejoicing that was! How could we ever have doubted our miracle working Lord?

✳ ✳ ✳ ✳

Scripture References:
   Luke 10:38–42; John 11:1–44; John 12:1–3

Spiritual Reflections:
   "O Lord, grant that I may desire Thee, and desiring Thee, seek Thee, and seeking Thee, find Thee, and finding Thee, be satisfied with Thee forever."   —Augustine

   "Once His gifts I wanted, now the Giver own; once I sought for blessing, now Himself alone." —A. B. Simpson

Suggested Hymns:
   • "Sitting at the Feet of Jesus"
   • "More Love to Thee, O Christ"

A Samaritan Woman

Come, all you who are thirsty, come to the waters (Isaiah 55:1).

My heart was heavy as I made my midday trip to Jacob's Well at the edge of our village of Sychar (SI-kar). Somehow my life had not turned out the way I would have liked it to be. My continual search for contentment and happiness always seemed to end in disappointment or further confusion. My mind was occupied with these concerns as I approached the well. It seemed unusually quiet for that time of day.

Suddenly I was startled by the sight of a stranger sitting calmly nearby. I tried to study Him. Although He seemed weary from the heat of the day, there was a certain composure and kindness in His face. His clothing and appearance made Him look different from the other men in our village. I wondered about Him. No doubt a Jew, I supposed, passing through Samaria.

My thoughts were interrupted by His gentle voice. To my surprise He asked, "Will you give me a drink?"

Pausing a moment, I answered scornfully, "You are a Jew and I am a Samaritan woman. How can you ask me for a drink? Since ancient times the Jews have not associated with us because of our opposing religious practices."

"If you knew the gift of God," the stranger continued, "and who it is that asks you for a drink, you would have asked Him and He would have given you living water."

Confused by His statement, I made an attempt to appear bold and indignant. "Sir, you have nothing to draw with and the well is deep. Where can you get this living water? Are you greater than our father Jacob, who gave us this well and drank from it himself as well as his sons and cattle?"

Kindly, but with a voice of authority, the stranger replied,

"Everyone who drinks this water will be thirsty again, but whoever drinks the water I give him will never thirst. Indeed the water I give will become in him a spring of water, welling up to eternal life."

"Oh, sir," I cried, "give me this water so I won't get thirsty and have to keep coming here to draw water!"

At that the man turned and fixed His eyes on mine tenderly. "Go call your husband and then return."

Fearful and ashamed, I stammered, "I have no husband."

His piercing gaze was steady as I tried to look away. "You are right when you say that. The fact is you have had five husbands, and the man you now have is not your husband."

I gasped in astonishment. How could this stranger . . . and a Jew . . . know all this about me? Yet His manner was not harsh or accusing, only compassionate and understanding. "Sir," I replied, "I can see that you are a prophet." Then attempting to distract Him, I added, "Our fathers worshiped on this mountain, but you Jews claim that the place we must worship is in Jerusalem. Which is right?"

Gently He responded, "Believe Me, woman . . . the time is coming and has now come when the true worshipers will worship the Father in spirit and truth. . . . God is a spirit, and His worshipers must worship in spirit and in truth."

I was deeply stirred by His words and manner. I paused a moment. "I know that Messiah is coming. When He comes He will explain everything to us."

Then the stranger declared, "I who speak to you am He!"

I gazed at Him in awe and embarrassment. A feeling of utter shame for my past life swept over me. I should have known, I chided myself, for not only did He already know everything about me, but He did not condemn me. He merely seemed to be pleading with me to believe what He said and to fully trust Him. As I stood silently before Him, He smiled tenderly at me as if He forgave all my sins and understood all my concerns.

Just then a group of His friends returned and gathered around Him. The men, who carried bundles of supplies and food, stared at me in curiosity but said nothing. Leaving my water pot, I turned from them and ran. Breathlessly I reached the village, calling excitedly to everyone along the way, "Come see a man who told me everything I ever did. Can this be the Christ?" And as a large number of our people hurried to the well to see this stranger, I knew in my heart that He was truly our long-awaited hope—God's promised Messiah.

I was filled with a joy and peace that I had never known before. My Lord had given me a new life . . . His living water . . . so that I need never thirst again!

＊ ＊ ＊ ＊

Scripture Reference:
   John 4:1–42

Spiritual Reflections:
   Consider anew the significance of the Lord's instruction to the Samaritan woman about true worshipers (John 4:21–24). What are some of the practical implications of this truth as applied to our worship practices today?

> "Give me to drink, I pray."
> He saw the bitter, broken heart
> And longed to impart His everlasting rest.
>
> Refreshing she sought—and found Him who
>   is the Fount of Life;
> The true and living Way.
>
> Within her soul gushed forth that hour a
>   spring of hope divine,
> And into her poor darkened heart the light of
>   heav'n did shine.
>
> —author unknown

Suggested Hymns:
   • "Fill My Cup, Lord"
   • "Springs of Living Water"

Drama 40

Pilate's Wife

My guilt has overwhelmed me like a burden too heavy to bear (Psalm 38:4).

How unhappy I felt whenever it was necessary for me to accompany my husband Pilate to this Province of Judea. As a Roman administrator, he was assigned here to be governor. To me this region seemed strange and turbulent without all the entertainment and lavish lifestyle of Rome. Often I complained to Pilate of my boredom and discontent, but his problems as a ruler of the tempestuous Jewish people have kept him much too occupied to devote any time to my needs.

One day as I relaxed in our Jerusalem palace overlooking the crowded city below, I glanced out of our wide windows for a little diversion. My curiosity was stirred by the sight of a large crowd gathered in the square. The people were intently watching a man in their midst who was stooping over a cripple on the ground. All at once the lame man was lifted to his feet and began to leap around with no help. I was astonished! The cheers and exclamations of the crowd could be heard as they followed the healer down the road. Several times after that I caught glimpses of that same healer. How serene and kind He looked as He performed other amazing miracles. At times He simply sat patiently teaching the people or even gathering children around Him lovingly. Who was this unusual man, I wondered? After questioning my servants, I learned that He was Jesus, a traveling prophet from Galilee.

As time went on, I often thought about that healer-prophet. I heard that He spoke as no man ever had spoken . . . foretelling strange events to come and teaching about an all-powerful God, His heavenly Father, who is able to forgive sins. This was all very new to me since, as a Roman woman, I believed in many gods. I heard that the prophet took time

148

to help anyone who needed Him, even the least important person. I began to feel a deep desire to know more about this man . . . perhaps to talk with Him and try to understand the truths He was teaching.

The Holy Feast of the Passover arrived. Pilate and I had come to Jerusalem to see that order was maintained among the masses of Jewish people who had streamed into the city. I was secretly hoping that I might find a way to see the strange prophet when He came to celebrate the Passover. Of course, I did not mention this to Pilate as he was much too busy with his own affairs; he would never understand my interest in a Jewish teacher.

The night before the Feast, my servants came to inform me that Jesus had been arrested by the Jews for preaching that He was their promised Messiah. This was blasphemy, the Jewish leaders charged. They wanted Jesus sentenced to death and were planning to trick my husband and make him responsible for condemning this man. My servants reported that the prophet's life was in grave danger.

That night I could not sleep for thinking about Jesus. Even though I had never met Him, I was convinced from all the reports that He was a good man, certainly not worthy of a cruel death. He had helped so many people and had done no harm to anyone. As I lay tossing on my silk-covered bed, I was tormented by thoughts of Him. I tried to form crude prayers to the God of the Jews, whom I did not know . . . asking that this good man be spared from these hysterical people. But then I began to laugh at my foolishness for becoming so upset by the fate of an itinerant Jewish prophet who was causing an uprising among His own people. Soon I drifted off to sleep.

A startling dream awakened me! I sat up in panic and alarm. The dream was about this Jesus . . . about who He really might be . . . and what judgment would await those who brought harm to Him. I was trembling and shaken. I felt that I must take action before it was to late. I must warn Pilate. Quickly I arose and penned a note to my husband, who was now in the judgment hall with the Jewish leaders. I instructed the messenger to deliver my note immediately to Pilate. I had written, "Do nothing, I beg of you, to that innocent man Jesus, for I have been deeply troubled this morning because of a dream about Him."

I stood by the open window, staring into the pre-dawn darkness with a strange feeling of apprehension. Why had I not talked to Pilate sooner about this good man? Why had I lacked the courage to speak out in His behalf? And why had I not gone out to find this prophet and get to know Him while I had the opportunity? Perhaps then I might have had a greater influence on my husband and the frenzied crowd that was now accusing Jesus.

I began to hear shouting and turbulence from the judgment hall. Then the chant of the howling mob grew louder and more insistent. I leaned through my open window in the dim morning light to hear them more clearly. I buried my head in my arms as the raucous mob shouted: "CRUCIFY HIM! CRUCIFY HIM! LET HIS BLOOD BE UPON US AND UPON OUR CHILDREN! CRUCIFY, CRUCIFY . . ."

My tears fell freely as I turned away with utter remorse. I had been too late!

❊ ❊ ❊ ❊

Scripture References:
    Matthew 27; Mark 15; Luke 23; John 18; Acts 3:13

Spiritual Reflections:
    Tradition states that Pilate ended his life by suicide and that his wife, Procula, later professed Christianity.

Suggested Hymns:
    • "Were You There?"
    • "What Will You Do With Jesus?"

Drama 41
Mary Magdalene

I will be glad and rejoice in Your love, for You saw my
affliction and knew the anguish of my soul (Psalm 31:7).

How painful it is to recall my early life and the kind of
person I once was! I was known by all to be demon
possessed. I lived with uncontrolled anger and violent
outbursts, often screaming and thrashing about. I no longer
had the will or the ability to restrain my wild actions. My
condition seemed hopeless.

Then one day an unusual man passed through our little
town of Magdala (MAG-da-la) on the western shore of the
Sea of Galilee. I noticed the crowd that quickly gathered
around Him. Drawing closer to observe, I was startled when
this stranger called Jesus suddenly moved toward me and
looked directly into my face. He spoke gently and seemed
to understand fully my desperate need. As He began to
explain His message of love and forgiveness and the need to
trust in Him, I could not take my eyes from His
compassionate face. The bonds of my dreadful condition
began to melt away. My heart was filled with a peace and
joy I had never known before. I became a new person! I
knew I would forever be grateful to this Jesus of Nazareth
for reclaiming me from my shameful, sinful state.

I became one of Jesus' devoted followers. My fervent desire
was to introduce Him to others who also needed to hear His
life-changing message. Sharing my goods and money, I tried
to contribute to the daily needs of Jesus' disciples. I joined
with the other women who stayed near our Lord to offer
whatever assistance they could.

As time went on, more and more people believed our
Master's message and became His followers, especially when
they saw His marvelous deeds and miracles. My devotion
and desire to serve Him continued to grow. I wanted only to

151

be the kind of person He would have me be. But then, at the very height of Jesus' ministry, just when we all hoped that He was about to establish a glorious kingdom of peace and justice on earth, tragedy devastated us. Hateful religious leaders in Jerusalem charged our blessed Lord with blasphemy and convinced the Roman rulers that He was guilty of death by crucifixion. We were shocked and confused! But on that day of sadness, we women and the disciple John determined not to forsake our Master. We followed closely as He was led in a procession to Golgotha and there nailed to a shameful cross between two thieves. How our hearts were breaking as we stood weeping beside Jesus' mother and heard our Lord's final cry, "Father, into Thy hands I commend My Spirit!" Never had I felt such despair.

We watched numbly as some of His followers carried His limp form to an empty tomb. The other women and I worked frantically to prepare His body for a proper burial since it was nearly the beginning of the Sabbath when we could no longer work. Finally, I returned to my home, anguished and dejected.

I was anxious to do even more to express my deep gratitude for all my dear Lord had meant to me. I obtained some new spices and arranged to return with several of the other women to complete the burial process. Early on Sunday morning as the first rays of light began to appear, we ran to the tomb with our supplies. Sadly, I moved into the garden ahead of the others. Fond memories of our beloved Jesus . . . His goodness, tenderness, and kindness . . . filled my mind. He had delivered me from such darkness and had transformed my ugly life to one of usefulness and joy. How I mourned for Him!

I reached the tomb before the others . . . but no guards were there . . . no stone . . . an empty tomb! I was stunned. Then in terror and amazement, I ran swiftly to find Peter and John where they were sleeping. "They have taken the Lord out of the tomb," I cried, "and we don't know where they have put Him." Running hurriedly back to the grave together, we saw the linen burial clothes lying there and the rock-bed empty. Astonished, Peter and John hastened to spread the news to the other disciples while I remained behind.

Weeping in sorrow and despair, I moved closer again to the tomb. I was startled to see two angels in white seated at the head and the foot of the slab where Jesus' body had been placed. "Woman, why are you crying?" they asked.

I sobbed, "They have taken my Lord away and I don't know where they have put Him!"

As I looked away, another figure stood near me. "Woman, why are you crying? Who is it you are seeking?"

Assuming this was the gardener, I pleaded somewhat indignantly, "Sir, if you have carried Him away, tell me where you have put Him and I will get Him." My tears fell even more freely.

Then I heard His gentle voice . . . "Mary."

"Master . . . My Lord!" I cried. Deep joy filled my despairing heart. The darkest night had suddenly turned to the brightest day. Jesus, our Lord and Master, was alive!

✳ ✳ ✳ ✳

Scripture References:
   Mark 16:9; Luke 8:2–3; John 20:1–18

Spiritual Reflections:
   A formerly demon-possessed woman became the first person to announce Christ's resurrection.

> They came to the quiet garden in the early
>   morning gloom,
> And there in the shadowed darkness they
>   found an empty tomb.
> Their hearts were heavy-laden, bowed with
>   deep despair;
> But when they lifted tear-dimmed eyes, lo,
>   Jesus was standing there.
> So oft in the midst of sorrows when hope
>   seems cold and dead,
> With lifted eyes, we too may see an empty
>   tomb instead.   —author unknown

Suggested Hymns:
   • "In the Garden"
   • "Lead Me to Calvary"

Drama 42

Jairus (JA-i-rus)

How great is Your goodness which You have stored up
for those who fear You (Psalm 31:19).

As leader of the local synagogue, I was well known in our
little village on the Sea of Galilee. My responsibilities
included conducting the weekly worship service— selecting
those who were to lead the prayers, read the Scripture, and
do the preaching. My work was enjoyable and rewarding,
and life was going well for our family. But without warning,
my only daughter, the pride and joy of my life, suddenly
became very ill. Our local doctors were increasingly baffled
as each day she became worse until she lay close to death.
My wife and I were devastated, not knowing where to turn.

Then a friend told me that the young prophet from
Nazareth had crossed the lake and had arrived on our shores.
We had heard many reports about this man called Jesus—
how He taught wonderful truths about God and helped
people wherever He went. As a Jewish leader I normally
would not have sought this kind of help, but I was desperate!
I sensed that my daughter's only hope for survival was a
supernatural miracle.

So that same day I hastily made my way to the large
crowd gathered about Jesus there on the seashore. Pushing
my way toward Him, I humbly dropped to my knees and
pleaded earnestly, "Master, my little daughter is at the point
of death. Please come and lay Your hands on her so that she
may get well and live!"

Jesus turned to look at me . . . with such compassion in His
face . . . and told me to lead the way to our home. As we
hurried along the dusty road, the large crowd began following
and pressing in on Him. It seemed that everyone was trying
to touch Him. Soon I saw a frail looking woman reaching
frantically toward Jesus until she was able to grasp the edge

of His cloak. How amazed we were to hear Him say, "Who touched Me?" Then looking tenderly at the poor person trembling at His feet, Jesus said, "Daughter your faith has made you well; go in peace, and be healed of your affliction."

I was astonished when this woman with the wasted body got up and moved about with new vitality. The crowd began praising Jesus. But inwardly I was resentful that He would spend so much time on a chronically ill older woman when my lovely twelve-year-old daughter so desperately needed His help. At that moment a friend from home came running up to tell me, "Jairus, your daughter is dead. Don't bother the teacher any more."

My life collapsed! My daughter had meant everything to me. But I heard Jesus say calmly, "Don't be afraid . . . just believe, and she shall be made well." When we arrived at our home, Jesus sent away everyone except three of His disciples, my wife and me. Inside the house many friends were weeping loudly and lamenting my daughter's death. Seeing them, Jesus commanded, "Stop weeping for she has not died, but is asleep." The friends burst out with scornful laughter and looked at Him as though He were insane.

Taking no notice of them, Jesus quietly approached my daughter's bed. He paused a moment, then said, "My child, get up!" To our amazement, instantly my daughter's spirit returned, and she stood upright. Jesus told us to give her something to eat, and what a joyous meal that was! My precious daughter was alive again and well.

Before leaving, Jesus insisted that He didn't want us telling anyone what had happened. But it wasn't long before the news of this amazing miracle spread rapidly throughout our entire region.

Since that day I have been doing some serious thinking. Could this Jesus possibly be the long-awaited Messiah about whom we read and study each Sabbath in our synagogue worship?

✳ ✳ ✳ ✳

Scripture References:
    Matthew 9:18–26; Mark 5:21–24; 5:35–43; Luke 8:41–56

Spiritual Reflections:

> Doubt sees the obstacles—
>   Faith sees the way.
> Doubt sees the darkest night—
>   Faith sees the day.
> Doubt dreads to take a step—
>   Faith soars on high.
> Faith questions, "Who believes?"
>   Faith answers, "I."
>   —author unknown

"Faith is to believe what we do not see, and the reward of faith is to see what we believe."   —author unknown

"The more clearly we see the sovereignty of God, the less perplexed we are by the calamities of this life."
                        —author unknown

Suggested Hymns:
- "Simply Trusting Every Day"
- "Hiding in Thee"

A Woman Who Was Healed

Listen to my cry, for I am in desperate need; rescue me!
(Psalm 142:6).

How miserable I was. All hope seemed gone! For twelve long
years I had been ailing with a chronic blood disorder, too
weak to do much at all. Many physicians had prescribed
various remedies for me, but nothing had made me well.
Then one day I heard of a prophet—Jesus of Nazareth—who
did miraculous deeds. They said He cured sick people like
me with a mere touch of His hand, and even the blind and
demented ones were healed by Him. I fervently believed that
finding a way to meet this man would be my only hope.

When news came that this prophet had just returned to
Jerusalem, I set out to find Him. Before long I came upon a
great crowd moving along the dusty road. In the midst I
could see several men attempting to restrain the people from
jostling a serene looking man who must be this Jesus. I knew
that somehow I had to reach Him. But with the pushing and
shoving of the clamorous crowd and the darting of children
back and forth, it seemed like an impossible task.

Standing under the blistering sun, I felt weary and faint.
Desperately I began to push my way forward into the moving
mass. I dodged between flailing arms and stumbled on. At
times I tripped over someone's feet, but I kept struggling
toward the place where the prophet stood. Then suddenly I
caught a glimpse of Him just a few feet ahead of me. With
all my remaining strength, I thrust myself forward and fell
in a heap behind Jesus Himself. I panicked as I saw Him
begin to move forward. Quickly I stretched out my hand
and lightly touched the edge of His cloak.

Abruptly Jesus stopped and asked calmly, "Who touched
Me?" The friends surrounding Him said they had not noticed
anyone. One of His helpers reminded Him that the people

were all crowding and pressing against Him. Yet Jesus insisted, "Someone touched Me . . . I know that power has gone out from Me."

I was terrified . . . but I knew I could not hide from Him. Trembling and excited . . . for I could feel the new vitality and strength in my body already . . . I knelt at His feet. I explained to Him and the surrounding crowd the misery of my illness and my desperate need to touch His garment. With tears of joy I rose up and announced to all that I had now been healed!

Jesus gazed at me with such a look of tenderness and understanding that all my fear disappeared. I fixed my eyes on Him in awe and wonder as I heard Him say, "Daughter, your faith has healed you. Go in peace." I went my way with a new vigor, praising and worshiping my miracle-working Lord!

✳✳✳✳

Scripture References:
    Mark 5:24–34; Luke 8:42–48

Spiritual Reflections:

> She only touch'd the hem of His garment
>   as to His side she stole,
> Amid the crowd that gather'd around Him,
>   and straightway she was whole.
> "O touch the hem of His garment,
>   and thou, too, shalt be free!
> His saving pow'r this very hour
>   shall give new life to thee.   —George F. Root

"Prayer is releasing the energies of God, for prayer is asking God to do what we cannot do ourselves."
                                            —author unknown

Suggested Hymns:
   • "The Great Physician"
   • "I Believe in Miracles"

Salome (sa-LO-me)

Humble yourselves, therefore, under God's mighty hand
that He may lift you up in due time (1 Peter 5:36).

I must confess that I was always proud of my social position as
the wife of the admired and respected Zebedee (ZEB-e-dee).
With his many fishing boats, my husband was a prosperous
and successful man. I was also very proud of our two sons,
James and John, for their intelligence and abilities. We had
given them careful guidance, and they had never disappointed
us. I knew that I was the envy of many women here in
Capernaum (ka-PUR-na-um), our lovely village on Lake Galilee.

It was somewhat perplexing to my husband and me when
both of our sons announced one day that they were leaving
the secure positions in their father's business to become
followers of Jesus. He was the son of my sister Mary, and we
had known Him since His childhood. As time went on, we
began to realize that there was something different about this
young man. His teachings, which at first seemed so strange,
began to impress us and cause us to consider spiritual matters
much more seriously. Then there was the memorable day at a
family wedding when we all saw Jesus turn water into choice
wine. "Who is He?" we began questioning each other. "Is this
really Joseph's and Mary's son?"

Before long my two sons reported many other amazing
events they had witnessed as they traveled around with Jesus.
The sick and the lame were miraculously healed, thousands
were fed from a meager lunch, the blind received their sight,
and even the dead came to life at His command. More and
more we began pondering whether Jesus could actually be
the One foretold in Scripture—our long-awaited Messiah.
Perhaps my sons had made a wise decision in following
Him. I, too, began seeking out Jesus whenever He was in
our region of Galilee. I listened attentively to His teachings.

I also tried to minister to His needs whenever I could and sent generous contributions to His small band of disciples to assist in their ministry. Increasingly I became convinced that Jesus is truly the Son of God.

I was pleased that James and John were among the closest companions of the Master. The eternal kingdom He described to us was surely His own. In heaven, then, how exalted and honored my two sons would be. From time to time, I would overhear discussions and even arguments among the disciples concerning their places in the heavenly kingdom. I began to think seriously about this myself. Certainly my sons deserved the most important places since they had·sacrificed so much to become followers of Jesus. Knowing that the disciples had never openly questioned the Master about this matter, I decided that I should be the one to bring about a frank discussion of it.

One day after the crowds had departed and Jesus sat peacefully resting, I approached Him, motioning for my sons to follow. I bowed respectfully and looked up at Him. "Lord, I have a certain thing to ask of You."

Turning kindly to me, He responded, "What is it you wish, Salome?"

I blurted out, "Grant that one of these two sons of mine may sit at Your right and the other at Your left in the heavenly kingdom!"

For a hushed moment Jesus looked at the three of us. Then calmly He replied, "You don't know what you are asking. Can you drink the cup I am going to drink or be baptized with the baptism I am baptized with?"

"Yes," my sons answered quickly, "we can!"

Gazing afar off, Jesus continued, "You will indeed drink from My cup, but to sit at My right or left hand is not for Me to grant. These places belong to those for whom they have been prepared by My Father." I heard the other disciples begin rebuking my sons for the boldness of our request. But Jesus quietly called the group together and explained, "Whoever wants to become great among you must be your servant . . . just as the Son of Man did not came to be served, but to serve, and to give His life as a ransom for many."

As I slipped away silently, I felt deeply ashamed. I knew

that my pride and ambition for my sons had been a foolish mistake. I will never forget the lesson Jesus taught us that day about humbly serving Him.

I continued to be devoted to the needs of the Master and accompanied Him and His disciples whenever I could. Then, without warning, came those dark and terrifying days of Jesus' trials and crucifixion. With Mary, His mother, I stood at the foot of the cross in confused and devastating sorrow. What could this mean? Our faith in the Master began to waver.

Then on the morning after the Sabbath, I went with Mary Magdalene and the other Mary to our Lord's tomb, to anoint His body for proper burial with the special spices we had prepared. But what a sight greeted us—an empty tomb! When a young man nearby proclaimed loudly, "He is risen!" we were stunned! Bewildered and afraid, we stumbled out of the garden. Only when meeting the disciples later that day were we assured that the startling news was indeed true. Jesus had appeared in their midst while the doors were closed. What indescribable joy filled my heart!

Our Lord was truly alive again, and my pride and ambition have been replaced by a humble desire to serve and honor Him.

✳ ✳ ✳ ✳

Scripture References:
   Matthew 20:20-28; 27:55–56; Mark 15:40; 16:1–8; John 19:25

Spiritual Reflections:
   "Pride slays thanksgiving, but a humble mind is the soil out of which thanks naturally grows. A proud person is seldom a grateful person, for he never thinks he gets as much as he deserves."   —Henry Ward Beecher

   "What we do for ourselves dies with us. What we do for God and others is immortal."   —author unknown

Suggested Hymns:
   • "When I Survey the Wondrous Cross"
   • "Living for Jesus"

Drama 45

Cleopas (KLE-o-pas)

> This bread is My flesh, which I will give for the life of
> the world (John 6:5).

I had gone to Jerusalem one week early to keep the Passover
and hopefully to see Jesus, our teacher and beloved Master.
I was filled with expectation and joy during my two hour
walk from our quiet little village of Emmaus (e-MA-us) to
the bustling big city. I believed so strongly in this man . . . in
what He taught and how He helped people. I was certain
that He was truly our promised Messiah, who was about to
establish His new kingdom of love and justice for us.

And then those never to be forgotten events occurred so
quickly: our Lord's arrest, the mock trials, that hysterical
crowd, betrayal by one of His trusted friends, the gruesome
scourging, and then that cruel death upon a Roman cross.
Our hopes and dreams were completely shattered!

Three days after the crucifixion the entire city still seemed
to be disturbed about what had happened. There was even
a rumor circulating that Mary Magdalene and some of the
other followers had gone to the tomb on Sunday morning
and found it empty. They claimed they were told by angels
that our Lord had risen. But I didn't put much faith in such
wild reports. Later I met a friend from home and told him
that I'd had enough of the turmoil and had decided to return
to our peaceful village to escape the eerie gloom I felt in
Jerusalem. He agreed to join me.

As my friend and I walked along slowly, we began
reviewing all of the events we had experienced during those
past few days. Soon, however, we were overtaken by a
kindly, rather young looking man, who asked if He might
join us. My friend and I continued our earnest conversation
without paying much attention to this person.

After a few minutes the stranger asked what we were

discussing that made us look so sad. "Are you a visitor to Jerusalem," I replied impatiently, "and do not know the things that have happened there in these past days?"

"What things?" He asked politely.

"About Jesus of Nazareth!" we both blurted out. "He was a prophet, powerful in word and deed before God and all the people. But the chief priests and our own rulers handed Him over to Rome to be sentenced to death . . . and they crucified Him! We had so hoped that He was the one who was going to redeem Israel."

Then to our surprise, this stranger calmly began explaining the truths of the Old Testament. He told us that these Scriptures clearly taught that a Savior would be born, that He would suffer and die for the sins of mankind, that God would raise Him from the grave, and that He would then go to His Father in heaven. One day He would return to establish His eternal kingdom. Never had I heard the Scriptures so clearly and powerfully explained. This stranger knew every detail in the writings of Moses, David, Isaiah and all the other prophets.

By this time we were nearing our village and it was quite late. The stranger said farewell and began to leave us, but my friend and I were so overcome by His teachings that we wished to hear more. We hurried after Him and urged Him to join us for an evening meal. He graciously consented.

We were about to begin eating our humble supper when the stranger took a piece of bread, gave thanks, broke it into pieces, and offered it to us. We saw the wounds in His hands. Instantly we knew it was our Lord! We dropped to our knees in worship . . . but He disappeared from our sight.

Our meal was no longer important. Never had I experienced such a thrilling but awesome moment! We ran almost all the way to Jerusalem to tell the disciples what had happened. We found them and other close followers gathered together. As soon as they saw us, they shouted with joy, "Jesus is alive and has already shown Himself!" They listened with rapt attention as we told them of our encounter with the Living Lord and all that He had taught us on the way to our home.

Until my dying breath, I will never forget that Resurrection Sunday and the burning I felt in my heart on that evening walk to Emmaus with the risen Lord. His praise will forever be on my lips!

                    ✻ ✻ ✻ ✻

Scripture References:
    Mark 16:12; Luke 24:13–25

Spiritual Reflections:

> Yes, life is like the Emmaus road,
>   and we tread it not alone,
> For beside us walks the Son of God,
>   to uphold and keep His own.
> And our hearts within us thrill
>   with joy at His words of love and grace,
> And the blessed hope that when day is done,
>   we shall see His blessed face.
>   —Avis B. Christiansen

"The antidote for occupation burnout is a 'burning heart' for God."   —author unknown

Suggested Hymns:
    • "Abide with Me"
    • "Revive Us Again"

Dorcas

He who is kind to the poor lends to the Lord, and He will reward him (Proverbs 19:17).

The gift of life is truly a miracle . . . and since Almighty God in His bountiful love destined me to live a second time, my gratitude and devotion to Him are beyond expression. Now my greatest desire is that others might glorify God through my life.

My Hebrew name Tabitha (TAB-i-tha) means "gazelle"— a graceful and beautiful animal. In Joppa where I live, however, the language spoken is Greek, so I am called Dorcas. Our city is a busy seaport on the coast of the Mediterranean Sea, and various nationalities come here to live. Many years ago the prophet Jonah fled from the Lord on a sea voyage from here.

One day a noted spiritual leader named Peter came to Joppa to tell us about Jesus, the promised Messiah. Our lives were changed. I joined many others in becoming a faithful follower of Christ. From then on I yearned to find some way to show my love for the Lord.

Often as I sat near an upper window in my comfortable home overlooking the water, I could see beggars clutching their rags against the chilling sea winds. Also playing about the narrow streets were unkempt looking boys and girls; many of these were orphans or the children of widows whose husbands had been lost at sea. My heart was stirred by these sights. One day the Lord showed me clearly how I might serve Him. I was a skilled seamstress. I could make garments for these needy ones and at the same time tell them about Jesus. I gathered together all the material and usable clothing I could find. Soon the word spread through the town that anyone in need could come to me for decent garments.

Women and their children began arriving at my home in

such great numbers that I worked feverishly day after day and often far into the night. I always provided food for those who were hungry. While earnestly trying to express to each one the good news about Jesus our Savior, I often became so occupied that I scarcely took time for my own nourishment.

One day as I sat sewing and conversing with the women and their little ones, I suddenly felt very dizzy. A severe pain in my head and neck gripped me as I stumbled to a nearby couch. The concerned cries of the others became gradually dimmer until soon my world was totally black. My next awareness was that of a distant voice calling me by my Hebrew name. Then again I heard it, this time forcefully commanding, "Tabitha, rise up!" Opening my eyes, I was startled to see our spiritual leader Peter standing by my side. As I stared at him in surprise, he took my hand and helped me to my feet. I realized that I had been placed in one of the upper rooms of my home and that my body had already been prepared for burial. But now my pain and dizziness were completely gone, and I felt well and strong again!

After Peter called to my many friends gathered below, they hurried to my room. They stared at me for a moment, then rushed in to rejoice and embrace me. "She's truly alive again," they cried repeatedly. I realized that they had all come to mourn my death, but now their dirge had turned to joyous praise. My loving Lord had given me a new life!

Throughout the entire city of Joppa, the thrilling news of my restored life spread rapidly. Many of those who heard of this amazing miracle responded to the love of Jesus our Lord. Now my desire is to use this new life even more than before in serving Him by serving others. I want to express my gratitude with loving deeds of mercy. My daily prayer is that my new life—like my name itself—may truly be something beautiful for the glory of our great God!

✳ ✳ ✳

Scripture Reference:
   Acts 9:36–43

Spiritual Reflections:

Scripture records only eight people, including Jesus, who were raised from the dead.

The story of Dorcas teaches that soul winning and social responsibility are woven intrinsically together and constitute an inherent part of any ministry. A total ministry to the whole person includes soul, body, mind, and spirit.

"People don't care how much you know until they know how much you care."

—author unknown

You are writing a gospel, a chapter each day,
   By deeds that you do, by words that you say.
Men read what you write, whether faithless or true,
   Friend, what is the gospel according to you?

—author unknown

Suggested Hymns:
- "Brighten the Corner"
- "Where Cross the Crowded Ways of Life"

Drama 47

Paul

My message and my preaching were not with wise and persuasive words . . . .so that your faith might not rest on men's wisdom but on God's power (1 Corinthians 2:4–5).

"The life I live in the body, I live by faith in the Son of God, who loved me and gave Himself for me." This has been my testimony ever since that day on the Damascus Road when I was dramatically changed by God. Now the sole passion of my life is to know personally the resurrected Christ and to proclaim His life-changing message to others. I am driven by a consuming desire to win converts to Him—Gentiles as well as Jews—and to organize them into local assemblies—the body of Christ. I make every effort to encourage and instruct these new congregations in their worship of God by making them understand the marvelous Gospel of grace as it is revealed in our Lord.

But this certainly was not the goal of my early life. I was a Jew, but because I was born in the Greek city of Tarsus (TAR-sus), a renowned center of education and philosophy, I was a citizen of that city as well as a citizen of Rome. Later my family moved to Jerusalem. There I received a thorough education in the Old Testament Scriptures as well as the ancient classics from Rabbi Gamaliel (ga-MA-li-el), the eminent Pharisee and teacher of the Law. Soon I became obsessed with a desire to stamp out that fanatical "sect" known as Christians. I believed that they were insane zealots who were completely blasphemous as they went about preaching that Jesus, their Master, had actually risen from the grave and ascended to His Father in heaven. In fact, the purpose for my trip to Damascus was that I had heard about a large group of these devout followers residing there. I was determined to have them arrested and brought back to our council in Jerusalem. Before leaving Jerusalem, however, I got caught up in an unusual event. I witnessed the stoning of Stephen. He was one of those young Christian zealots who had stirred up our Jewish people with his very persuasive preaching. He was brought before the Jewish council of leaders and convicted of blaspheming against Moses and God. The witnesses took this young man outside the city walls and began hurling stones at him. Somehow I ended up holding the cloaks of these witnesses while the stoning was taking place. But I was shaken by Stephen's final words, "I see the heavens opened, and the Son of Man standing at the right hand of God." And even while he was dying, his face shone as though it were the face of an angel! I was never able to forget this.

As we traveled along that Damascus Road, I really felt that I was honoring God by trying to eliminate those "followers of the way," as they liked to call themselves. In the midst of my hateful thoughts, suddenly a dazzling light from heaven blinded me. A heavenly voice warned me that it was really Jesus whom I was persecuting. I fell on my face in fear and readily confessed my sin. I humbly acknowledged Christ as the Lord and Master of my life. When I stood up, I trembled as I realized I could no longer see. The friends who had accompanied me on this journey had to lead me into Damascus, where I remained for the next three days without any nourishment. How grateful I was when one of the devout believers from the city, a godly man named Ananias (AN-a-NI-as), visited me. When he arrived, he was fearful since he had heard of the havoc I had inflicted on his fellow believers in Jerusalem. Yet he placed his loving hands on my head and said, "Brother Saul," which was my Jewish name, "the Lord Jesus, who appeared to you on the road as you were coming here, has sent me so that you may see again and be filled with the Holy Spirit." Immediately a film fell from my eyes and I could once again see! I was given food to regain my strength and later was baptized as a believer in Jesus Christ.

I felt compelled to spend some time by myself in the lonely Arabian desert. It was here that the Holy Spirit first revealed to me the mysteries of the Gospel of grace. I saw clearly that the Mosaic Law I had so fervently studied and defended was now perfectly fulfilled in the person and redemptive work of Christ. I also realized that all people—Jew, Gentile, male, female, slave or free—are equal in God's sight. Each of us must respond with personal faith to the mercy and grace of our Lord if we are to be accepted by the heavenly Father. Nothing good we do will ever merit God's favor or fit us for heaven. It is only the atoning work of Christ that saves the human soul.

I returned to Damascus, where I preached these truths in the synagogues and proclaimed boldly that Jesus is truly the Son of God. The people were baffled when they heard me preaching this way. They recalled so well my former background. Eventually, many became very angry with my ministry and even threatened my life. In fact, if it had not been for some of my Christian friends who helped me escape from Damascus, I might have been killed.

After I made my way to Jerusalem, I tried to unite with the disciples, but many were still fearful and suspicious of me. It was Barnabas who first spoke on my behalf, telling of my changed life and of how I had preached Christ fearlessly while in Damascus. After that I was able to remain for a brief time and share in the ministry with these brethren. Soon, however, I had to make another escape from the city to avoid the growing hatred and threats of those Jerusalem Jews.

In the years that followed, my ministry for the Lord has been fruitful and rewarding. I traveled by land and sea to nearly every major city in the Mediterranean world, preaching Christ and establishing churches. But it was never an easy task. I was beaten, stoned, imprisoned, shipwrecked, left adrift at sea, and often suffered thirst and hunger. There was also a special weakness that God allowed me to endure . . . a constant reminder of my human frailty and my need to depend on His divine help alone. But through it all, the Lord has stood by my side and given me the strength I needed so that His message of grace might be fully proclaimed for all to hear.

Since that day on the Damascus Road when I first met the Lord, I can say with all truthfulness that I have never been ashamed of His Gospel. I realize that it alone is the power of God for the salvation of everyone who believes. My earnest prayer is that with all boldness Christ shall be exalted in my body, whether by life . . . or by death.

✻✻✻✻

Scripture References:
Acts 7:58; 9; 21:39; 22:3; 26:4–5, 10–11; 28; 2 Corinthians 11:21–33; Galatians 1:17

Spiritual Reflections:
Paul's conversion occurred about A.D. 34. His first missionary journey was about A.D. 46. After the Lord Jesus, the apostle Paul was the most influential voice in the early history of Christianity. He is the author of at least thirteen New Testament books.

Tradition states that Paul was beheaded at Rome about A.D. 67–68 during Nero's reign.

"Let us recognize our inadequacy without Christ—our invincibility with Him." (Relate this to the apostle Paul's statement in Phil. 4:13.)   —author unknown

And shall I use these ransomed powers of mine
    For things that only minister to me?
Lord, take my tongue, my hands, my heart, my all—
    And let me live and love for Thee!

—author unknown

Suggested Hymns:
- "Amazing Grace"
- "I Know Whom I Have Believed"

Drama 48

Timothy

Fan into flame the gift of God which is in you (2 Timothy 1:6).

I grew up in a religiously divided household with a Jewish mother and a Greek father. Yet I was strongly influenced in my early life by the deep faith in Jehovah that my mother Eunice and grandmother Lois had. Each day during my childhood they taught the Scriptures to me. Then while I was still in my teens, it was announced that a noted preacher of the Christian faith was coming to our town of Lystra to minister to a small group of converts living there. My mother, grandmother and I were curious to know more about this new teaching of which we had heard many favorable reports. We learned that the preacher was Paul, a former Jewish religious leader but now a zealous follower of Jesus Christ. Paul's powerful message revolved around the death, resurrection and ascension of Jesus into heaven. We were inspired and enlightened with these truths and began to understand that Jesus is truly the fulfillment of all our Old Testament teachings. Gladly we pledged our faith to Christ and surrendered our lives to His Lordship.

After my conversion to Christianity, I developed an intense desire to learn everything possible about this Gospel of grace and to share its message of love and forgiveness with everyone. Within a short time, the leaders of our local assembly recognized my unusual interest in spiritual matters. With the laying on of hands, I was ordained for the ministry of preaching. Some time later, the apostle Paul returned to Lystra. He, too, recognized my pastoral gifts by confirming my ordination. I was invited to join his group as they traveled throughout the Mediterranean region establishing local congregations in the Christian faith.

As we traveled and worked, I continued to learn more

about the Christian doctrines and the role of a local church—the pillar and foundation of truth in this world. The beloved apostle and I were constant companions. He often referred to me as his "son in the faith." When he was unable to visit a particular church, he would send me in his place to minister and teach. His special concern was always with the leadership of each congregation. I was to urge pastors to preach continually the essential doctrines of the Gospel, and I was to caution every leader to live a life that honored the cause of Christ. While instructing these local church leaders, however, I often experienced feelings of insecurity, since I was generally much younger than they. But then I would receive a note of encouragement from the beloved apostle with words such as these: "Don't let anyone look down on you, Timothy, because you are young, but set an example for the believers in speech, in life, in love, in faith and in purity." Another time he sent me this needed reminder: "God did not give us a spirit of timidity, but a spirit of power, love and self-discipline."

On one occasion the apostle sent me to oversee the church leaders in Ephesus. In these churches serious problems had developed, including the rise of false leaders, who were discounting the teachings of the apostle Paul. This was truly a difficult time for me. Again the advice and encouragement of my spiritual mentor were so helpful to me. He reminded me to avoid disputing over that which is minor and to simply preach the true faith with a good conscience, always supporting my ministry with fervent prayer, free from malice or anger toward anyone.

While involved in giving spiritual guidance to these churches in Ephesus, I received another letter from the beloved apostle with the sad news that he had been imprisoned in Rome for preaching the Gospel. He indicated that his time had now come for departing from this life. It was so disheartening to hear him say that all of his friends except Luke had deserted him during this time. Yet he quickly added that the Lord had stood by his side and given him strength. In spite of his hardship, Paul still thought about my pastoral ministry and offered this final advice: "Preach the Word; be prepared in season and out of season;

correct, rebuke and encourage with great patience and careful instruction."

The apostle also requested that I make the long journey to Rome to have one last visit with him before winter set in. How can I do less for this man of God, my spiritual father, who has meant everything to me?

✳ ✳ ✳ ✳

Scripture References:

Acts 16:1–3, 12; 17:14; 19:22; 20:3–6; 2 Corinthians 1:1; Philippians 1:1; Colossians 1:1; 1 Thessalonians 1:1; 3:2; 2 Thessalonians 1:1; 1 and 2 Timothy; Philemon 1 (1 Timothy was written by the apostle Paul about A.D. 64, and 2 Timothy was probably the last letter written by Paul about A.D. 67.)

Spiritual Reflections:

Paul's letters to Timothy and Titus are known as the Pastoral Epistles. They provide important guidelines for the administration of local churches today.

Whether Timothy reached the apostle Paul before his death is conjecture. Some writers see in Hebrews 13:23 an indication that Timothy even shared in Paul's imprisonment.

According to tradition, Timothy continued to minister as the bishop of Ephesus until his death as a martyr.

Suggested Hymns:
- "Am I a Soldier of the Cross?"
- "Joy in Serving Jesus"

Titus

You show a fine loyalty in everything that you do for
these fellow Christians (3 John 5 NEB).

I was the first gentile helper used by the apostle Paul in his
missionary travels. When this fact became widely known
among many of his friends, they were deeply disturbed.
"How can this young full-fledged Gentile really understand
and teach the Gospel message?" these Jewish believers asked.
One day Paul and Barnabas took me to Jerusalem, where
this matter was debated at length. A subject of special
discussion was the practice of covenantal circumcision. Many
of the Jewish Christians were actually insisting that unless
gentiles were circumcised, they really could not be accepted
by God. Paul and Silas did not yield to these brethren but
told them plainly that they were attempting to destroy the
freedom found in Christ, putting believers once again under
legal bondage. The Jerusalem conference ended peacefully,
however, with the affirmation that gentile Christians would
not be required to be circumcised.

The apostle Paul continued to use me to minister to
churches whenever he was unable to do so. Often I was sent
especially to help settle problems that arose from time to
time. One such troublesome church was in Corinth. Paul
dearly loved these people, but even though he had spent
considerable time with them, many difficult problems had
recently developed. These included gross immorality,
quarreling, refusal to collect funds for needy saints, and even
the questioning of Paul's apostolic authority. With the Lord's
help I was able to work with these people and in time resolve
many of their problems. Paul was so pleased with my report
of progress that he is completing a second letter of instruction
and encouragement to them. The apostle wants me to
personally deliver it for him.

A short time ago, the apostle and I revisited the churches on the Island of Crete, the seat of an ancient and powerful civilization. The people here have long been known for their corrupt behavior. We found the churches in much disarray because of poor leadership. The apostle was unable to stay very long and asked me to remain and try to straighten out the unfinished problems. One of my first responsibilities was to appoint elders in each of the local assemblies and then to train them in their church duties and spiritual leadership. This was not an easy task. Being an overseer of God's work is always a demanding responsibility, and these Cretians are not naturally disposed to this kind of discipline.

Just recently I received from the beloved apostle a helpful letter intended to assist me in my ministry here in Crete. He gave some very specific guidelines for Christian leadership. The apostle emphasized that church leaders must always be blameless, hospitable, self-controlled, and able to encourage others with sound teaching. Paul also wisely urged me to be a model of such integrity and goodness among the people that even those who oppose our message will not be able to fault our lives. He further stated that I should avoid any form of foolish controversy. I must simply keep stressing this essential truth: "The grace of God that brings salvation has appeared to all men and teaches us to say 'no' to ungodliness and worldly passions, while we wait for the glorious appearing of our great God and Savior, Jesus Christ."

Paul wrote that he wants me to complete my work in Crete as quickly as possible so that I might join him for the winter at Nicopolis (ni-COP-o-lis), a rather lengthy journey from here. He will send several other helpers to carry on here while I am gone. The apostle also wants to send me to the church at Dalmatia (dal-MA-shah), which would mean another long and difficult journey. The work of the Gospel ministry is never ending!

✳✳✳✳

Scripture References:
The epistle to Titus; 2 Corinthians 2:13; 8:6, 16; 12:18; Galatians 2:3; 2 Timothy 4:10

Spiritual Reflections:

Titus was written about A.D. 65 by the apostle Paul to Titus, one of Paul's most reliable helpers.

Tradition states that Titus eventually returned to Crete, became the permanent bishop there, and died peaceably on the island at an advanced age.

"The best prize life offers is the chance to work hard at work worth doing."   —Theodore Roosevelt

"I will place no value on anything I have or may possess except in relation to the kingdom of Christ."
                                                            —David Livingstone

Suggested Hymns:
- "Work for the Night Is Coming"
- "I'll Go Where You Want Me to Go"

Drama 50

Philemon

Love is patient, kind . . . keeps no record of wrongs
(1 Corinthians 13:4–5).

I have been greatly disturbed by a letter I just received today
from the aged and beloved apostle Paul. For a number of
years this dear man of God has visited our home here in
Colosse (ko-LOS-ee) whenever possible. He has helped me
establish a small congregation of fellow believers, who meet
regularly for worship in my spacious manor. Our people
have come to truly love and respect this revered Christian
leader. We were saddened to learn that our dear brother
recently has been confined in a Roman prison for preaching
the Gospel. And while there in prison, he evidently has come
in contact with that former slave of mine, Onesimus (o-NES-
i-mus), who some time ago not only ran away unlawfully
from me but actually stole many of my priceless belongings.

I have been searching diligently for this runaway wretch.
I was determined that when I found him, I would make an
example of him that would long be remembered. But now
this letter from Paul has arrived. He states that while in
prison, Onesimus became a genuine believer in Christ and
is now so loved by Paul that he calls him a son. Then the
apostle continues by asking the other members of the church
and me not only to forgive this slave but actually to welcome
him into our fellowship as a Christian brother. Although I
have always tried to be kind, especially to other believers,
somehow this seems to be expecting too much of my
Christian charity.

Let me read to you some of the statements in Paul's letter:

Philemon—our dear friend and fellow-worker:

I am sending Onesimus back to you in person. I would

have liked to keep him with me so that he could help me while I am in chains for the Gospel. But I did not want to do anything without your consent, so that any favor you do will be spontaneous and not forced.

Perhaps the reason he was separated from you for a little while was that you might have him back for good—no longer as a slave, but better than a slave, as a dear brother. He is very dear to me but even dearer to you, both as a man and as a brother in the Lord.

So if you consider me a partner, welcome him as you would welcome me. If he has done you wrong or owes you anything, charge it to me—I will pay it back.

And one thing more: Prepare a guest room for me, because I hope to be restored to you in answer to your prayers.

The grace of the Lord Jesus Christ be with your Spirit.

(I have written this with my own hand.)

Paul

Onesimus should be arriving here at any moment. Can you understand why I am so distraught?

Help me, O Lord, to have Your spirit of love and compassion even as You accepted and forgave each of us. May I receive this brother as You would have me to do.

❋ ❋ ❋ ❋

Scripture References:
The epistle to Philemon; Colossians 4:9

Spiritual Reflections:
The epistle to Philemon was thought to have been written by the apostle Paul during his first captivity in Rome, A.D. 63 or early A.D. 64.

The Bible does not tell us how the master received his returning slave. It is generally believed, however, that Philemon did accept and forgive Onesimus as Paul had requested.

The gathering of believers in the house of a wealthy member was characteristic of the early church.

"It is manlike to punish but Godlike to forgive."
—P. von Winter

"Bear with the faults of others as you would have them bear with yours. Be patient and understanding. Life is too short to be vengeful or malicious. Life is too short to be petty or unkind."   —Phillips Brooks

"Forgiveness is not a case of 'holy amnesia' that wipes out the past. Instead, it is the experience of healing that drains the poison from the wound."   —author unknown

Suggested Hymns:
- "O To Be Like Thee"
- "More Like the Master"

Jude

A false witness will not go unpunished, and he who pours out lies will not go free (Proverbs 19:5).

Though I have become quite well known throughout this region as the younger brother of James, the respected leader of the home church in Jerusalem, and also of Jesus, our Lord Himself, I much prefer to be remembered simply as Jude, "a servant of Jesus Christ." Since the time following the resurrection—when I fully realized that Jesus is truly God's anointed Messiah—the goal of my life has been to serve and represent Him . . . to share His life-changing message with others and to build up my fellow believers in the holy faith.

I intended to complete a letter I was writing to all the local assemblies in this region. I wanted to encourage these followers of Christ with a reminder of the blessed salvation we enjoy by being united with our Lord. Before finishing my letter, however, I received shocking news concerning a devastating heresy that recently became rampant in many of our local churches.

It has been reported that some evil-minded adversaries of the faith have infiltrated these churches and have denied the authority of Jesus Christ as our only sovereign Lord and Master. As is true whenever a person's thinking becomes corrupt, these godless leaders live immoral lives and actually teach that the grace of God allows this kind of perverted behavior. This false teaching must be exposed!

When I received news of the godless and immoral people who had crept in among the congregations, I became so grieved that I felt compelled to write a message of warning instead of my original letter. I hurriedly informed my fellow believers about this dreadful heresy, encouraging them to remain steadfast in the faith they were taught by the Lord's apostles. This meant that each person must be absolutely firm in the essential truths of the Gospel, aggressively opposing those who would distort this faith.

I shudder when I think about the terrible punishment that awaits the wicked leaders who deceive God's people. The Scriptures are filled with examples of those throughout history who have defiled the grace of God in this way. For such people only the blackest darkness has been reserved forever!

It really should not have come as a surprise to me that this kind of heresy would develop in the churches. Our Lord's apostles have often warned that in the last times there would be scoffers who would follow their own desires, seek to thwart the redemptive work of Christ, and cause division among the believers. These evil leaders merely follow their own base instincts since they do not possess the true Spirit of God in their lives.

In order to avoid succumbing to such heresies, each individual believer must be actively engaged in those spiritual activities that continually build him up in the blessed faith . . . always praying in the power of the Holy Spirit and living with the glorious hope of our Lord's appearing. In the meantime, however, we must show pity for those who have been led astray and try to rescue them from evil corruption.

So again, beloved friends, I plead with you to stay close to the only One who is able to keep you from falling and to present you before His glorious presence without fault and with great joy—to the only God our Savior be glory, majesty, power and authority, through Jesus Christ our Lord . . . now and forevermore!

✳ ✳ ✳ ✳

Scripture Reference:
The book of Jude, written about A.D. 65–68

Spiritual Reflections:
The fact of Jude's family relationship to Jesus as a brother has often been questioned. However, Matthew 13:55 and Mark 6:3 definitely seem to support this. Also, see Galatians 1:19—"James, the Lord's brother."

What are some of the major spiritual heresies rampant today about which the evangelical church must be earnestly concerned?

"The world at its worst needs the church at its best."
—author unknown

Lord, how delightful 'tis to see
    A whole assembly worship Thee!
At once they sing, at once they pray;
    They hear of heaven, and learn the way.

Jesus, where'er Thy people meet,
    There they behold Thy mercy seat;
Where'er they seek Thee, Thou art found,
    And every place is hallowed ground.
—Isaac Watts

I love Thy Church, O God!
    Her walls before Thee stand
Dear as the apple of Thine eye,
    And graven on Thy hand.
—Timothy Dwight

Suggested Hymns:
- "The Church's One Foundation"
- "How Firm a Foundation"

Drama 52

John (Revelation)

Blessed is the one who reads the words of this prophecy
(Revelation 1:3).

After our Lord's ascension to heaven, I remained for some
time in Jerusalem with several of the other disciples, teaching
and preaching the Gospel. Eventually I felt compelled to
move to Ephesus. I desired to assist the believers there who
had suffered much persecution from Nero (NIR-o), that cruel
Roman emperor. After Nero's death and just when we
thought conditions might improve for the Christians, another
vicious emperor, Domitian (do-MISH-an), came to power.
He, too, demanded to be worshiped as a god. Since our
fellow Christians refused to do this, Domitian did his best to
eliminate them. He eventually heard of my resistance to him
and the influence I had in the churches throughout the Asia
Minor region. The order was given for me to be banished to
the Isle of Patmos, a bleak and rugged island in the Aegean
(e-JE-an) Sea.

While I was in exile there on Patmos, an Angel of God
enveloped me one Lord's Day, and I was caught up in my
spirit into heaven itself. How my soul thrilled with
exultation at what I saw and heard! God revealed to me
events that would take place soon as well as those in the
distant future. He told me to begin by writing to the seven
churches throughout my region with encouragement as
well as words of warning and rebuke. How our fellow
believers needed the reassurance that regardless of life's
persecutions, God will one day be their righteous ruler
and eternal king.

As I continued gazing around heaven, I saw a Lamb,
looking as if it had been slain, standing in the center of the
throne. Before the Lamb was a great multitude from every
tribe, language, people and nation. I heard them cry out

184

with a loud voice: "Salvation to our God who sits on the throne, and to the Lamb!" After that I heard the voices of thousands of angels loudly singing: "Worthy is the Lamb, who was slain, to receive power, wisdom, honor, glory, and praise!"

Then the Lord God showed me a new heaven and a new earth He had prepared for His people. I saw the Holy City, the new Jerusalem, coming out of heaven from God, prepared as a bride beautifully dressed for her husband. And I heard a loud voice from the throne saying: "Now the dwelling of God is with men, and He will live with them. They will be His people, and God Himself will be with them and be their God. He will wipe every tear from their eyes. There will be no more death or mourning or crying or pain, for the old order of things has passed away. Behold, I am making everything new!"

Finally, I was told to write these words, which are trustworthy and true: "I am Alpha and Omega, the Beginning and the End. To him that is thirsty I will give to drink without cost from the spring of the water of life. I will be his God and he will be My son, and surely . . . I come soon!"

Overwhelmed by the glories of heaven and the eternal destiny awaiting the people of God, I readily responded, "Even so, come Lord Jesus."

The grace of the Lord Jesus be with God's people everywhere.

✳✳✳✳

Scripture Reference:
    The book of the Revelation, written about A.D. 95 during the rule of Nero (A.D. 54–68) when the first real persecution of Christians began. From A.D. 81–96, during the rule of Domitian, another period of severe persecution for Christians ensued.

Spiritual Reflections:
    The author is the apostle John, writer of the fourth gospel and the three epistles bearing his name. Tradition states that John was released from Patmos after one year and

returned to Ephesus where he continued to minister until his death at an advanced age. He was the last of the original twelve disciples

The ultimate triumph and eternal reign of Christ is a thrilling finale to all of God's inspired Holy Scriptures.

Suggested Hymns:
- "All Hail the Power"
- "Jesus Shall Reign"

Performance Notes

Performance Notes

Performance Notes

Performance Notes

Other Music Resources by Kenneth W. Osbeck

Amazing Grace: *366 Hymn Stories for Personal Devotions*
An inspirational daily devotional based on 366 great hymns of the Christian faith. Each day's devotional highlights biblical truths drawn from the true-life experiences behind the writing of these well-known hymns. Each story contains a portion of the hymn itself, as well as suggested Scripture readings, meditations, and practical applications. Your personal or family devotional time will be enhanced by the challenging and inspiring thoughts contained in this thrilling collection of classic and contemporary hymn stories.
ISBN   0-8254-3448-3   400 pp.   paperback

52 Hymn Stories Dramatized
Some of the most well-known hymns of the Christian faith come alive with vibrant, true-to-life stories of their writing presented in dramatic form. These dramatized hymn stories add a new dimension to worship services and provide a vehicle for understanding the history of the hymns and their authors.
ISBN 0-8254-3428-9   144 pp.   paperback

101 Hymn Stories
(Foreword by J. Stratton Shufelt.) The true-life experiences and inspirational background stories behind 101 favorite hymns. Excellent for devotional reading, and sermon illustrations as well as for historical or biographical research. Includes the complete hymn with each story.
ISBN 0-8254-3416-5   288 pp.   paperback

101 More Hymn Stories

(Foreword by Cliff Barrows.) The stories behind the hymns of 101 additional past and contemporary favorites with the music included. An important companion volume to *101 Hymn Stories*.
ISBN 0-8254-3420-3   328 pp.   paperback

Devotional Warm-ups for the Church Choir

A variety of forty-three brief, challenging devotionals on ten different musical topics. Designed to provide spiritually stimulating material for church choir members, both individually and as a group. Pertinent group discussion questions as well as accompanying Scripture reflections are provided for each study.
ISBN 0-8254-3421-1   96 pp.   paperback

The M

A pract   local church
minist
ISBN   paperback

Pocke

A help   l knowledge
design   ains a useful
glossar
ISBN (paperback